I0805098

The most sublime mystery in the Christian faith is the incarnation of God in Christ. "The Word became flesh and blood, and moved into the neighborhood" (John 1:14), as Eugene Peterson's memorable translation puts it. Now Derek Vreeland has adapted *The Message* translation to lead us in a biblical exploration of the incarnation, crucifixion, and resurrection in a fresh way for small groups and individuals alike.

BRIAN ZAHND, author of *The Wood Between the Worlds*

Derek has accomplished something rare with the God in the Neighborhood Bible Studies. His work is rich and deep, saturated in Scripture and theologically sound, yet it also reveals a profound attention to the condition of our hearts. Through heartfelt prayers and spiritually attuned pastoral leadership, Derek invites us into the all-important work of Christlikeness. God in the Neighborhood is sure to deepen our affection for Christ and exhort us to enjoy closer fellowship with our incarnate, crucified, and risen Savior, Jesus.

KAT ARMSTRONG, Bible teacher, podcast host, and author of the **Storyline Bible Studies** series

Vreeland artfully guides us into Scripture's wild country, where we see with fresh eyes the wonder of the human God.

WINN COLLIER, pastor, director of the Eugene Peterson Center for Christian Imagination, and author of *A Burning in My Bones: The Authorized Biography of Eugene H. Peterson* and *Love Big, Be Well*

With theological depth and pastoral warmth, Derek Vreeland leads us into Scripture using the down-to-earth beauty of *The Message* translation to reveal the wonder of God made flesh. What I love most about this study is how it keeps our eyes on Jesus—God with us—and at the same time helps us imagine how that truth reshapes how we live with and for our neighbors. It is prophetic and hopeful, grounded and transformative.

JULIET LIU, pastor of Life on the Vine Christian Community

Derek Vreeland serves as a thoughtful guide in this excellent Bible study. I especially appreciate the way each lesson is structured in four sections, offering space for journaling and prayer. It's a rich resource—perfect for personal reflection as well as group study.

TIM WILDSMITH, pastor, professor, YouTuber, and author of *Bible Translations for Everyone* and *Daily Scripture Guidebook*

In the God in the Neighborhood Bible Studies, my friend Derek Vreeland opens up the heart of the gospel not as a collection of abstract doctrines but as the truth of God to be lived every moment, every day, wherever we are. *Incarnation* reveals God drawing near. *Crucifixion* displays God's self-giving love. *Resurrection* announces that hope is stronger than despair. These studies are grounded in the story of Scripture, pastoral in tone, and deeply practical. Derek writes as both a pastor and a friend, guiding us gently toward Jesus. As you work through these studies, you will find that God is not only in heaven above us but also alive in the laughter, sorrows, and stories of the place you call home.

TOMMY BROWN, author of *The Speed of Soul*

As Christians we know that Jesus is the face of God (2 Corinthians 4:6), which means that every contour of the Scripture is but the outline of the face of the incarnate, crucified, and resurrected one; the one in whom is all the fullness of the Godhead (Colossians 2:9), in whose presence we melt in adoration and worship. We believe this—but sometimes it is difficult to see. We need wise guides to help us not only recognize his face but also hear his voice and follow him where he goes—into the country of sin and death to seek and save the lost. I commend to you this series by Derek Vreeland—biblical, accessible, pastoral, wise. A resource that will edify believers old and new.

ANDREW ARNDT, lead pastor at New Life East and author of *A Strange and Gracious Light*

Writing a good resource on the crucifixion of Jesus is difficult to do. It probably doesn't seem that way at first; what could be more quintessential to Christianity than a Bible study on the death of Jesus? But this is precisely what makes it difficult. These discussions have been had so often—and had so poorly—that we tend to push them away. But Vreeland has given us something reliable here in this work. This study doesn't manipulate the reader or cheapen the story of Jesus' death. It helps us relate to the power of the crucifixion in our concrete experience and apply it to our own lives. Jesus moved into the neighborhood, and we already live in one! Vreeland helps us see why this matters.

MARTY SOLOMON, author of *Asking Better Questions of the Bible* and creator of *The BEMA Podcast*

# CRUCIFIXION

GOD IN THE NEIGHBORHOOD BIBLE STUDIES

8 Lessons on How God Saves Us

DEREK VREELAND

NavPress

Published in alliance with Tyndale House Publishers

NavPress.com

*Crucifixion: 8 Lessons on How God Saves Us*



A NavPress resource published in alliance with Tyndale House Publishers



The Team:
David Zimmerman, Publisher; Olivia Eldredge, Acquisitions Editor; Elizabeth Schroll, Copyeditor; Lacie Phillips, Production Assistant; Eva M. Winters, Designer; Sarah Ocenasek, Proofreading Coordinator



For information about special discounts for bulk purchases, please contact Tyndale House Publishers at csresponse@tyndale.com, or call 1-855-277-9400.

ISBN 978-1-64158-988-8

Printed in the United States of America

32 31 30 29 28 27 26
7 6 5 4 3 2 1

*To Taylor*

*May your wishes all come true*

# CONTENTS

The Word became flesh and blood,
    and moved into the neighborhood.
We saw the glory with our own eyes,
    the one-of-a-kind glory,
    like Father, like Son,
Generous inside and out,
    true from start to finish.

JOHN 1:14

# AS WE BEGIN

*An Introduction to Crucifixion*

The cross remains the central symbol of our faith because Jesus' death on the cross is at the heart of what Christians believe. As the apostle Paul declares in Romans, "God put his love on the line for us by offering his Son in sacrificial death while we were of no use whatever to him" (Romans 5:8), and love is what prompted the Word to move into the neighborhood. We have been given access to God's neighboring presence not because of any righteous action of our own but because of the precious blood of Jesus shed for us: "It was a perfect sacrifice by a perfect person to perfect some very imperfect people" (Hebrews 10:14).

Jesus died for us to both rescue and reveal. The blood of Jesus *rescues* us from all the corrupting power of sin, hell, and death. And the cross *reveals* the nature of God and the very essence of the Kingdom of God. At the cross we see King Jesus

- not conquering but going down in defeat,
- not killing his enemies but being killed,
- not shouting but silenced,
- not thriving but suffering,
- not retaliatory but forgiving,
- not triumphant but disgraced,
- not glorious but hideous,
- not exalted but humiliated,
- not celebrated but mocked,
- not grandiose but pitiful,

- not regal but repulsive, and
- not revered but ridiculed.

Through his death, Jesus shows us the heart of God the Father. The cross reveals that the Kingdom of God comes through cosuffering love. Crucifixion is not how rulers take their thrones—it's how criminals meet their doom. Yet we can only understand the depths of the meaning of the cross by looking at it through the resurrection. If the gospel ended with the cross, it wouldn't be good news at all. The resurrection of Jesus changes how we see the cross (but that is the subject of book 3 in this Bible study series). The task before us in these lessons is to see *who God is* and *how God saves us.*

God could have chosen to save the world in any way God wanted, but the God of infinite power and might chose to save us by moving into the neighborhood, becoming one of us, and joining us in death through a hideous death of his own and then joining us in new life by rising from the dead. This unimaginable way of saving the world shows us what God is like. God is cosuffering, and God's love is self-giving. From the vantage point of the resurrection of Jesus, we see the cross as the center of everything—the center of the Kingdom of God; the center of God's rescuing, revealing, and restoring work; and the center of God's new world! But it isn't the cross alone. The saving work of Jesus begins with his virgin birth. Jesus' birth saves us from isolation. His cross saves us from sin. His resurrection saves us from death. All these actions work together in a beautiful act of redemption . . . and the cross remains at the center of it all.

The lessons in this Bible study explore the mystery of the crucifixion, God joining us in death to set us free. This study fits well with the season of Lent, particularly Holy Week and Good Friday, but it can be used at any time during the year. We begin in the Old Testament with Psalm 22, a psalm of David that speaks prophetically of the crucifixion of Jesus. This lesson leads us to the next one as we consider the words of Isaiah 53 regarding the then-forthcoming suffering of Israel's king. From here we move on to the New Testament, to the Gospel of Matthew, where Jesus reveals the purpose in his impending death, not by lecturing his disciples but by serving them a meal with bread and wine.

From our lesson in Matthew, we push on in the New Testament with stops in Romans, Ephesians, Hebrews, 1 Peter, and 1 Thessalonians. The Spirit-inspired writers of these letters reflect on the meaning of Jesus' death, emphasizing themes of God's love, the welcoming of non-Jewish people into God's covenant family, Jesus as the new and better High Priest, and healing found in the wounds of Jesus. We find not one way to think about the implications of Jesus' death for us but rather a variety of ways in which Jesus' blood rescues us and reveals God's love to us. We are invited to bring our woundedness to the wounds of Jesus, where we find healing and new life.

---

This Bible study series uses the beauty and sacredness of ordinary language found in *The Message*, a contemporary and imaginative translation of the Bible, to lead you on a journey through the Scriptures to encounter Jesus in his life, death, and resurrection. The series is broken into three parts:

Book 1, *Incarnation*, dives deep into the mystery of the incarnation, where God meets us, joining us in life.

Book 2, *Crucifixion*, reflects on Jesus' execution, where God joins us in death, and in doing so, saves us.

Book 3, *Resurrection*, leads us on an Easter journey, where God joins us in life anew to restore us to what we were created to be: image bearers of the God of love.

When we realize that God is with us in life, we *come alive*. When we understand that God is with us in death, we *believe*. When we experience God-With-Us in new life, we *participate*. These studies are designed to bring you into "God's neighboring presence," a phrase I picked up from Eugene Peterson.[1] The coming of Jesus marks God moving into our neighborhood, and he is present with us as personally as any of our neighbors.

## How to Use This Bible Study

Lessons in these Bible studies are designed for either individual reflection or group study in small groups, Sunday school classes, or home groups. You are invited to use these Bible studies for your own personal growth and spiritual formation. Lessons are made up of four parts—"The Approach," "The Word," "The Neighborhood," and "The Prayer." Here is how each lesson is structured.

*The Approach: Setting the Scene*

We begin with an introduction to the Scripture passage from *The Message* we will cover in each lesson. "The Approach" ends with starter questions to get you thinking (if you are reading on your own) or to help your group begin sharing with one another.

*The Word: Diving into Scripture*

Following our introduction and opening questions, we turn our attention to a particular passage of Scripture and dig in, looking at the uniqueness of the language of *The Message*. In his translation, Eugene Peterson sought to break down the dividing wall between so-called secular and so-called sacred language. For Peterson, *all* language is sacred because it is all a gift from God.[2] Questions are provided here, as well, to encourage you to enter the text more fully.

*The Neighborhood: Living It Out*

We will wrap up each lesson by looking outward toward our own neighborhoods, asking how the passage of Scripture calls us to live in the way of Jesus while we are among our real flesh-and-blood neighbors. Following Jesus is not merely gaining knowledge and categorizing God facts. Following Jesus is a way of living shaped by the Holy Spirit around the death and resurrection of Jesus so that our lives look like dying to self and rising to reflect the life of Jesus. Reflection questions guide this outward focus on how we live in our neighborhoods filled with real people who may or may not identify as Christians.

*The Prayer: Drawing Near to God*

Each lesson concludes with a prayer drawn from the specific Bible passage used in that lesson.

There are companion videos available on my website here:

## Before You Start

If you are using these Bible studies on your own, find a quiet and comfortable place to read. Before you start a lesson, take a deep breath, exhale slowly, and offer a brief prayer. Ask the Holy Spirit to work with Holy Scripture to show you the ways of Jesus. As you are reading, feel free to jot down responses to the questions throughout each lesson.

If you are using these Bible studies in a group, take turns introducing yourself to the group; perhaps you could each share why you are in this Bible study or what you hope to get out of it. Open with prayer, asking Jesus to pour out the Holy Spirit on your group so that the Holy Spirit will be your teacher and guide. Identify a group leader to guide the conversation. Give people a few moments to reflect on the questions through the study, and then invite them to share with the group their thoughts and answers to the questions. Don't rush people to answer. Trust and learn from silence.

Whether you're doing this study on your own or in community, if you are able, read all Scripture passages out loud and pray the prayer at the end of each lesson aloud.

I love Jesus. I've loved Jesus since I was fifteen years old, and after all these years, I *still* love Jesus, because he never ceases to amaze and surprise me. And I love leading Bible studies, because when we take time to study Holy Scripture, God always surprises me with new details that make me ponder. My prayer is that you will grow in gratitude through these Bible studies and see with greater clarity what God has done for us in and through Jesus. I pray you will grow in your knowledge of the ways of Jesus and feel the nudging of the Holy Spirit to live out what you believe.

*Derek Vreeland*
*Lent 2025*

LESSON 1

# I NEED A NEIGHBOR

## The Approach

I got bitten by a snake once, a *poisonous* snake, while camping alone in the back-country, and instead of hiking out of the woods, I went to sleep.

In September 2021, I was hiking solo on the Eagle Rock Loop nestled in the Ouachita National Forest in western Arkansas. I started hiking around two o'clock in the afternoon and didn't see any other hikers until I made camp near a creek four miles down the trail. Two young male hikers passed by as I was setting up my camp. We talked for a bit before they headed down the trail to camp near the parking lot where their truck was parked. I washed up in the creek and changed into dry clothes (my hiking clothes were soaked with sweat). I made a good-sized campfire as the sun was setting. After dark I realized I hadn't washed my feet, so I grabbed my headlamp and headed back to the creek.

My campsite was in a clearing about 150 feet down a spur trail right off the main trail. With my headlamp illuminating the way, I turned right to walk down the main trail to the creek. I slipped off my shoes, dipped both feet in the cool, flowing creek, and cleaned them as well as I could. I used a bandana to dry my feet, stood up, and started walking up the trail, looking left for the spur trail back to my camp. But there was a problem: I couldn't find it. I walked back down to the creek, adjusted my headlamp to the brightest setting, and started over. I slowly made my way up the main trail, shining my light to the left, looking for the spur trail . . . and again, I couldn't find it.

I walked back down to the creek and tried to remember how many steps I'd taken on the trail to the creek. I thought it had been fewer than twenty, so I quickly formulated a plan to take seventeen steps up the trail, turn left into the woods, and walk until I found the campsite. I started up the trail for a third time, counting each step. When I got to step seventeen, I turned left and started bushwhacking through the trees, hoping to catch sight of the reflective guylines on my tarp.

It turned out to be a solid plan, but before I could make it back to camp, it felt like my leg caught on a thorny bush. I shined my headlamp down, and to my surprise, I saw a snake slithering away from me. Noticing its half diamond–shaped markings, I immediately stepped back. It was a copperhead, an aggressive (and unfortunately, common) poisonous snake in that area. As the snake continued moving away from me, I looked down again and saw a single puncture wound just above my right ankle leaking blood down into my shoe.

I thought, surprisingly nonchalantly, *Hmm. I think I just got bit by a snake.*

It took no more than ten more steps before I was standing back in my camp. I grabbed my first aid kit, sat down next to what was left of my campfire, and cleaned the wound. I wiped off the blood, dabbed on some antibiotic, covered it with a bandage, and wondered what to do next. I knew it would take two hours to hike back to my car and I'd arrive after midnight. Then I'd need to drive for nearly an hour to find a twenty-four-hour emergency room. My leg near the puncture was not swelling and wasn't red, so I didn't think I was in immediate danger.

All alone in the dark, I offered a brief prayer for wisdom. At that moment I realized how nice it would be to have a neighbor in my camp. I thought about walking down the trail to ask if the two guys I'd chatted with earlier would drive me to a hospital, but it was getting late, and I didn't want to bother them. So I decided to go to sleep and hike out the next morning.

I woke up a couple of times during the night and shined light on my ankle. It still hadn't begun to swell and still wasn't red, so I took those as good signs.

At daybreak, I got up, tore down my camp, strapped on my backpack, and started the four-mile hike back to the car. As I walked, my foot started swelling, and by the time I'd gotten to my car and driven forty-five minutes to the nearest ER, it had become significantly swollen. After a round of tests, the ER doctor gave me good news: I had very little venom in my system and no infection. *I'd survive!*

I'd never panicked, never even felt pain, but I'd been alone in the woods. I would have benefited from sharing my camp with another hiker. It would have made finding the camp in the dark a lot easier! And it would have been helpful to be able to talk through my options after the snakebite. It would have been good to have a neighbor.

As we begin our journey of reflecting on the crucifixion of Jesus, we start in the Old Testament with Psalm 22, a prayer of desperation. David, the Spirit-inspired writer of this psalm, cried out to God for help, just as Jesus the Suffering Servant would do centuries later. In a moment of great distress, both men found themselves thinking, *I need a neighbor* (Psalm 22:11).

Before we look at the first twenty-one verses of Psalm 22, reflect on these questions.

1. Nearly everyone has a story involving a snake, bird, or four-legged outdoor critter. What's yours?

2. When in your life have you felt the most isolated and alone?

3. When have you experienced the kindness of a neighbor?

## The Word

Jesus came to bring the long and turbulent story of Israel to fulfillment. What God began with the call of Abraham, God fulfilled in Jesus through his birth, teaching, miracles, death, resurrection, and ascension. The story of Jesus, which we celebrate and proclaim, isn't a one-off, stand-alone, generalized story. It's the capstone of a much bigger story—the story of God's work on earth through a particular people at a particular point in history. Jesus himself told his disciples before his ascension, "Everything I told you while I was with you comes to this: All the things written about me in the Law of Moses, in the Prophets, and in the Psalms have to be fulfilled" (Luke 24:44).

Jesus' death and resurrection specifically—which he told his disciples would happen—serve as a fulfillment of the Law, the Prophets, and the Psalms. Jesus continued, "You can see now how it is written that the Messiah suffers, rises from the dead on the third day, and then a total life-change through the forgiveness of sins is proclaimed in his name to all nations—starting from here, from Jerusalem! You're the first to hear and see it. You're the witnesses" (Luke 24:46-48). Jesus' hideous death by crucifixion shocked his disciples, but it had been spoken of beforehand in places like Psalm 22. In this ancient prayer, we encounter real human sorrow and a longing for God's neighboring presence.

> God, God . . . my God!
> Why did you dump me
> miles from nowhere?
> Doubled up with pain, I call to God
> all the day long. No answer. Nothing.
> I keep at it all night, tossing and turning.
>
> PSALM 22:1-2

---

In an act often called the cry of dereliction, Jesus uttered the opening lines of Psalm 22 while suffering on the cross. In his immense agony, Jesus felt utterly abandoned by God, rejected and forsaken by his Father. Jesus' very human experience of feeling isolated reveals that while our emotions are real, they do not always communicate the truth about God to us. While Jesus *felt* alone, as if God had dumped him a million miles from nowhere, the truth, which Jesus knew, was that God the Father was—and is—always present.

> And you! Are you indifferent, above it all,
> leaning back on the cushions of Israel's praise?
> We know you were there for our parents:
> they cried for your help and you gave it;
> they trusted and lived a good life.

And here I am, a nothing—an earthworm,
something to step on, to squash.
Everyone pokes fun at me;
they make faces at me, they shake their heads:
"Let's see how GOD handles this one;
since God likes him so much, let *him* help him!"
PSALM 22:3-8

---

*The Message*, working to draw out the richness of the Hebrew language, translates the phrase "enthroned on the praises of Israel" (Psalm 22:3, NLT) as "leaning back on the cushions of Israel's praise," which highlights the seemingly accusatory and exasperated tone of a suffering man.

Jesus felt the crushing weight of accusation on the cross. During his crucifixion, soldiers mocked him, and the crowd reviled him. According to Luke's Gospel, "The people stood there staring at Jesus, and the ringleaders made faces, taunting, 'He saved others. Let's see him save himself! The Messiah of God—ha! The Chosen—ha!'" (Luke 23:35). He felt forgotten, as if God didn't care.

And to think you were midwife at my birth,
setting me at my mother's breasts!
When I left the womb you cradled me;
since the moment of birth you've been my God.
Then you moved far away
and trouble moved in next door.
I need a neighbor.
PSALM 22:9-11

---

God's presence—which had at one time been nurturing—could no longer be felt or seen by Jesus on the cross. It felt like God had moved out of the neighborhood and pain, scorn, and suffering had moved in next door instead. As he was dying,

Jesus had neighbors, two thieves crucified along with him, but these were not the neighbors he wanted. One extended nothing but contempt for Jesus and the other asked for remembrance, but neither offered Jesus any help. How could they? Feeling displaced and alone, Jesus longed for the neighboring presence of God, a neighbor who could alleviate his suffering.

> Herds of bulls come at me,
>     the raging bulls stampede,
> Horns lowered, nostrils flaring,
>     like a herd of buffalo on the move.
>
> I'm a bucket kicked over and spilled,
>     every joint in my body has been pulled apart.
> My heart is a blob
>     of melted wax in my gut.
> I'm dry as a bone,
>     my tongue black and swollen.
> They have laid me out for burial
>     in the dirt.
>
> PSALM 22:12-15

---

The mocking crowd surrounding Jesus on the cross, offering nothing more than jeers and contempt, looked like a herd of bulls poised for a stampede. Jesus felt excruciating pain during his crucifixion, a pain felt in every bone, muscle, joint, and organ. As blood leaked from his body, dehydration set in, causing Jesus to exclaim, "I'm thirsty" (John 19:28).

> Now packs of wild dogs come at me;
>     thugs gang up on me.
> They pin me down hand and foot,
>     and lock me in a cage—a bag

Of bones in a cage, stared at
  by every passerby.
They take my wallet and the shirt off my back,
  and then throw dice for my clothes.
PSALM 22:16-18

---

All four Gospel writers record the division of Jesus' clothes by casting lots, the soldiers playing some kind of ancient game of chance (see Matthew 27:35; Mark 15:24; Luke 23:34-35; and John 19:23-24). Jesus' executioners stripped him of his dignity, crucifying him as an unclothed bag of bones and torn flesh for the world to gawk at and revile.

You, GOD—don't put off my rescue!
  Hurry and help me!
Don't let them cut my throat;
  don't let those mongrels devour me.
If you don't show up soon,
  I'm done for—gored by the bulls,
  meat for the lions.
PSALM 22:19-21

---

The plea for help in Psalm 22 is palpable. Jesus felt his life flowing out his body in tears of anguish and blood from open wounds. Death had sunk its sharp teeth like iron spikes into Jesus, ready to devour him. Jesus knew his body would not hold up, and still help was nowhere to be found. As he loudly uttered, "Father, I place my life in your hands!" (Luke 23:46), he took his last breath, trusting in a God who did not rescue him in that moment.

This psalm presents us with several jarring references to suffering and pain. Take a deep breath, and then take a moment to reflect on the following questions.

4. What are the differences between God the Father abandoning Jesus the Son on the cross and Jesus *feeling* abandoned?

5. Has there been a time when you've endured suffering and there has seemed to be no one there to help? How did that feel or how do you imagine that would feel?

6. Were you ever ridiculed or mocked during your childhood or teen years? How did you respond or how might you have responded?

7. What would it have been like to be Jesus in the darkest hour of his suffering?

8. In that moment on the cross, how did Jesus muster up faith amid suffering?

## The Neighborhood

In our age of increasing technology, we have more forms of digital communication than ever, and yet many people admit feeling lonely and isolated. We pull the car into the garage and close the door, never giving our neighbors the chance to say hello. We speed toward the door of the apartment, hoping not to be caught in a casual conversation with other people living in the building. As an introverted pastor working in an intensely extroverted world, I understand! Nevertheless, we each live in a neighborhood where hurting people are suffering in silence. Certainly we have moments when we need a neighbor, and we can be sure that the people who live near us need a neighbor from time to time too.

9. What can you do to be aware of the neighbors in need where you live?

10. What are some tangible ways you can point your neighbors to our ever-present God, who is ready to help?

## The Prayer

As you reflect on the needs in your neighborhood or community, offer this prayer.

*Lord God, we thank you for your nearness and closeness, especially in moments of pain and stress. We confess that often it feels like you have dumped us off millions of miles away from you. We also confess that we believe you are here, in this moment, by the Spirit, to guide and comfort us. May we perceive your merciful presence and have opportunities to point others to you. In Jesus' name, amen.*

LESSON 2

# LIKE A LAMB TAKEN TO BE SLAUGHTERED

## The Approach

I cannot quite wrap my head around how awful the death of Jesus must have been.

The brutality and gore of Jesus' crucifixion seems like something out of a horror movie. I have no firsthand experience with the kind of bloodshed on display as Jesus suffered and died. I have never served in the military, so I haven't set foot on a battlefield. I am not a hunter, so I have never field dressed a deer in the backcountry. I have never been in an emergency room when doctors and nurses have been trying to stabilize a car-wreck victim. In fact, the only time I have ever fainted was when I saw my dad's blood drawn in the hospital when he was in extreme pain.

I was sixteen years old and had abruptly left work because I'd received the news that my dad had been taken to the hospital. I held his hand as he lay back on the hospital bed, his eyes closed in pain. A nurse arrived to take blood, and as I watched the glass vial fill up with it, the room began spinning. As I inadvertently began to slump over, Dad shouted my name. I lifted my head, and the spinning room became completely dark. Down I went with a thud. I remember some nurses talking to me as I slowly regained consciousness. When I asked what had happened, I was met with a gentle smile and the words "You fainted." The nurse helped me to a chair, and I felt a bit embarrassed. I'd driven to the hospital to be with my dad, to be strong for him. Little did I know that I could be somewhat squeamish at the sight of blood.

We often lose sight of how torturous crucifixion was in general and how shocking Jesus' death was in particular. We sing about the preciousness of the blood of Jesus in our worship gatherings, perhaps not imagining Jesus' blood spilling as he died. In her theological masterpiece *The Crucifixion: Understanding the Death of Jesus Christ*, Fleming Rutledge writes, "The hideousness of crucifixion summons us to put away sentimentality and face up to the ugliness that lies just under the surface. The scandal, the outrage of the cross, is commensurate with the offense and the ubiquity of sin."[1] In many corners of cultural Christianity, the cross has been overlaid with sentimental clichés sought to elicit heartwarming feelings. A more honest and historical look at the cross strips away all sentimentality.

The Roman executioners slaughtered Jesus much like meat-processing workers slaughter animals for the meat we buy in the grocery store. The cellophane around the meat prevents us from seeing the slaughter; our surface-level reflections on the cross do the same. The death of Jesus was brutal because sin at work in us is equally brutal. Jesus died a horrible death for our sin, and the hideousness of his death reveals the hideousness of not only the sin at work in us but also sin at work in the world around us. The good news for us is that while Jesus endured unimaginable suffering and pain, he did so to defeat the monster of sin.

Imagining Jesus' death with grotesque images can be emotionally challenging, but it's a helpful practice. We need to be confronted with the depth of human brokenness at the hands of sin. That context allows us to see the beauty of the gospel story, which is centered on the brutal death of an innocent man.

Isaiah helps us with this imagery. Isaiah's prophecies, written more than five hundred years before Jesus' earthly life, provide for us heart-moving metaphors that ground our reflection on Jesus' death in history.

Before we look at a handful of verses in Isaiah 53, reflect on the following questions.

1. How do you do around blood? Are you anxious when asked to submit to a blood draw at the doctor's office?

2. How does the hideousness of the cross reveal the hideousness of sin?

3. How do you feel about looking at a passage of Scripture filled with images and metaphors of brutality and violence?

## The Word

Isaiah the prophet brought a word of hope to the people of God, who had experienced the turmoil of invasion and the trauma of deportation to Babylon. God directed Isaiah to lift up his voice to encourage these captive and broken people:

> "Comfort, oh comfort my people,"
>     says your God.
> "Speak softly and tenderly to Jerusalem,
>     but also make it very clear
> That she has served her sentence,
>     that her sin is taken care of—forgiven!
> She's been punished enough and more than enough,
>     and now it's over and done with."
>
> ISAIAH 40:1-2

---

Hope would come to captive Israel in the form of God's servant. This servant would be bathed in God's Spirit and "bring justice to the nations" (Isaiah 42:1, NLT). In one sense Israel was God's servant (Isaiah 49:3). Yet this servant appears to be someone else, a "messenger bringing good news" (Isaiah 52:7), an individual who would be "exalted, tall, head and shoulders above the crowd" (Isaiah 52:13). But before the servant's exaltation, he would suffer and be humiliated, the last thing we'd expect of God's chosen messenger.

> Who believes what we've heard and seen?
>     Who would have thought GOD's saving power would look like this?
>
> ISAIAH 53:1

---

This exalted messenger would eventually be "disfigured past recognition" (Isaiah 52:14). He wouldn't have the rich, powerful, dignified appearance that people typically look for in someone with saving power. God's way of saving the world will always look strange in our eyes.

> The servant grew up before God—a scrawny seedling,
> a scrubby plant in a parched field.
> There was nothing attractive about him,
> nothing to cause us to take a second look.
>
> ISAIAH 53:2

Jesus embodied Israel's identity and mission and fulfilled the role of Israel's servant-messenger. He came to proclaim the healing and saving nature of the Kingdom of God. Nothing about Jesus' appearance attracted people to him. Jesus grew up the son of a carpenter from a working-class family. He grew up in nowheresville, Nazareth, a small Galilean village not known for producing great leaders.

> He was looked down on and passed over,
> a man who suffered, who knew pain firsthand.
> One look at him and people turned away.
> We looked down on him, thought he was scum.
>
> ISAIAH 53:3

Isaiah predicted what Jesus would experience—suffering, pain, mocking, and disdain. At Jesus' public crucifixion some people gathered to gawk and jeer, yet others could not look at the torture of an innocent man. Public executions via crucifixion had become commonplace throughout the Roman Empire, but the regularity of seeing crucified bodies did not remove the vulgarity of it.

> But the fact is, it was *our* pains he carried—
> *our* disfigurements, all the things wrong with *us*.

We thought he brought it on himself,
that God was punishing him for his own failures.

ISAIAH 53:4

---

In a world where many people believe in the overly simplistic and often mistaken axiom "Good things happen to *good* people and bad things happen to *bad* people," it would have been easy for followers of Jesus to fall into a role like that of Job's miserable comforters and blame Jesus for his execution and death.[2] It would be easier to understand God punishing Jesus if Jesus had committed some kind of wrongdoing, but Jesus never sinned. In his crucifixion, Jesus carried *our* pain, *our* shame, *our* brokenness, and *our* wrongdoings.

But it was our sins that did that to him,
that ripped and tore and crushed him—*our sins*!
He took the punishment, and that made us whole.
Through his bruises we get healed.

ISAIAH 53:5

---

It looked like God was punishing Jesus, but it was our sins that did that. Jesus certainly received punishment—Roman punishment. Moreover, sin, the harsh slave master, punished him. Jesus received the crushing blow, and the result is our healing. His bruises take away our sin and brokenness, leaving us redeemed and healed.

We're all like sheep who've wandered off and gotten lost.
We've all done our own thing, gone our own way.
And God has piled all our sins, everything we've done wrong,
on him, on him.

ISAIAH 53:6

---

Using the words of the beloved hymn "Come, Thou Fount of Every Blessing," we each could say that we're "prone to wander, Lord, I feel it, / prone to leave the God I love."[3] We have the propensity to wander off and leave behind God and the people of God we love so dearly. Jesus, our Good Shepherd, comes to lead us back to the Father's house. He also comes as our sacrificial Lamb, shedding his own blood for the forgiveness of our sins, which God piled on him in his suffering and death.

> He was beaten, he was tortured,
>     but he didn't say a word.
> Like a lamb taken to be slaughtered
>     and like a sheep being sheared,
>     he took it all in silence.
>
> ISAIAH 53:7

---

Sometimes silence can be like thunder. When people expect a furious rant in response to verbal and physical abuse, silence can be the most jarring response. Jesus refused to hurl insults at his torturers. He maintained silence. Can you imagine such courage wrapped in meekness? Can you imagine such constraint amid searing pain? Jesus, God's own Son and our Lord, was slaughtered like an animal, only breaking his silence to utter (among other things) a prayer: "Father, forgive them; they don't know what they're doing" (Luke 23:34).

> Justice miscarried, and he was led off—
>     and did anyone really know what was happening?
> He died without a thought for his own welfare,
>     beaten bloody for the sins of my people.
>
> ISAIAH 53:8

---

Through the injustice of Jesus' wrongful death came justification for us. Though Jesus wasn't treated right, this miscarriage of justice was the way God set us right.

Jesus suffered *for* us—and Jesus still suffers *with* us. He considered not his own well-being. The executioners mercilessly beat Jesus bloody for our sins, and in his suffering, Jesus drew near to those who suffer. He understands abuse. He understands violence. He understands ridicule and abandonment. Jesus understands, and by his blood he redeems and restores all who have suffered.

> They buried him with the wicked,
> threw him in a grave with a rich man,
> Even though he'd never hurt a soul
> or said one word that wasn't true.
>
> ISAIAH 53:9

---

Joseph of Arimathea took Jesus down from the cross and placed him in his own tomb. Joseph, a man of means, fulfilled the words of Isaiah here by this loan. (Spoiler alert: Jesus didn't stay in that rich man's tomb long.)

> Still, it's what GOD had in mind all along,
> to crush him with pain.
> The plan was that he give himself as an offering for sin
> so that he'd see life come from it—life, life, and more life.
> And GOD's plan will deeply prosper through him.
>
> ISAIAH 53:10

---

The redemptive death of Jesus was the plan of God all along. It appears to us that God crushed Jesus with pain, but as we see in Isaiah 53:4-5, it may have *looked* like God punished Jesus, but our sins did the punishing. God was not in the Roman executioners, making sure Jesus suffered. Rather, "God was in Christ, reconciling the world to himself, no longer counting people's sins against them" (2 Corinthians 5:19, NLT). Jesus' crucifixion was "the LORD's good plan" (Isaiah 53:10, NLT), and this plan would deeply prosper because of Jesus' glorious resurrection. Reconciliation and redemption show the prosperity of God's plan through the death and resurrection of Jesus.

Take a moment to reflect on the following questions.

4. What do you find strange about God's way of saving the world through the crucifixion of Jesus? What do you find moving about God saving the world through Jesus' death?

5. What are the problems with a "Good things happen to *good* people and bad things happen to *bad* people" outlook on life?

6. How does it feel to know that Jesus suffered *for* us and *with* us?

7. Where did Jesus get the strength to remain silent and not verbally attack those who were attacking him?

8. What does Isaiah communicate in Isaiah 53:1-10 that helps us understand how Jesus' death saves us?

## The Neighborhood

We can all relate to the adage "Be kind to everyone you meet because everyone is fighting a great battle." People all around us face various kinds of battles, many of which come from their own woundedness. We have physical wounds that other people can see, but more often we have hidden wounds that nobody can see—emotional abuse, damaged emotions, mental illness, anxious thoughts, insecurity, and self-loathing, just to name a few. Jesus moved into our neighborhood to join us in our suffering. He invites all of us to bring our wounds to his wounds so that we may be healed.

9. Without being intrusive, how can you become aware of the wounds carried by the people in your neighborhood?

10. Who do you know who needs God's healing, transforming, or rescuing power? Pause and pray for that person.

## The Prayer

In addition to praying for the people in your neighborhood who need healing, offer this prayer out loud in the presence of God.

*Lord Jesus, we love you. We draw near to you in your suffering, and we bring our suffering and the suffering of those in our neighborhoods to you. Bind our wandering hearts to you, O Lord, as we search and wait on you for the healing and transformation we seek. You died as a lamb; now lead us as a shepherd into wide-open spaces of redemption and reconciliation. All for your name's sake, amen.*

LESSON 3

# THIS IS MY BLOOD

## The Approach

I am a minimalist.

I don't hang on to much. But in my bedroom closet I have an old cigar box that I purchased at the estate sale after my wife's grandpa passed away in the late 1990s. It now holds various mementos from early adulthood, including a picture of my wife from our honeymoon, my seminary ID, a name tag from the telecommunications company I worked for during my seminary years, and a half-ounce disposable clear-plastic Communion cup. Honestly, I don't remember the exact service when I used that cup. But I do remember saving it to recall a meaningful time of celebrating Communion.

I don't normally have a sentimental attachment to things. I'm anxious around clutter and tend to throw things away. My mantra is "Give it away, donate it, or throw it away." But that little Communion cup is still around some thirty years later. It has zero monetary value, and yet it remains stowed away as a testimony to the powerful role Communion has played in my own spiritual formation. I didn't always feel this way about Communion, but after thirty-five years of intentionally following Jesus, I'm convinced that the sacrament of Communion is not only at the heart of Christian worship; it's at the heart of Christian discipleship.

When we come to the Lord's Table, we practice humility, self-reflection, contrition, and confession of sin. Just as the bread is broken, so our hearts are broken in vulnerability as we realize our ongoing need for a Savior to forgive us, break the power of sin, and cleanse us from the pollution and corruption sin has left in its wake. Just as wine is poured into a cup, so are our lives poured out as a living sacrifice through acts of obedience to King Jesus. We do not grow in Christlikeness without regularly practicing humility and vulnerability, which the process of coming to the Communion table provides every time we eat the bread and drink from the cup.

I deeply appreciate that I came to faith in a Baptist church and grew in the faith in my more formative years in a Pentecostal/charismatic context. But neither of those traditions typically emphasize the practice of Communion (also known as the Lord's Supper or the Eucharist). In the Baptist, charismatic, and nondenominational churches I attended in high school and college, we would only celebrate Communion every few months, sometimes less often. Leaders in these kinds of churches often claim that celebrating Communion in a less frequent manner keeps Communion special, and I have often heard that a weekly practice of Communion would cause it to become less meaningful. While I sincerely respect Christians who practice Communion less often, for me, approaching the Communion table weekly with sincerity and intentionality has not caused it to lose any of its sacredness or power. The kinds of meaningful moments I had at the Lord's Table as a high school and college student receiving Communion a couple of times a year have not been diminished in the weekly celebration of the Lord's Supper. Nearly every time I come to the Lord's Table these days, I experience something meaningful.

Almost all Christian traditions acknowledge the memorial nature of Communion. We come to the Table to remember Jesus' death as emphasized in Luke's Gospel (Luke 22:19) and in Paul's instructions to the Corinthian church (1 Corinthians 11:23-26). Recalling Jesus' suffering and death in the practice of Communion is holy and helpful as a practice of discipleship, but it is only the beginning. When we eat the bread and drink from the cup, we not only remind ourselves—and proclaim to others—that Jesus died for us; we also remind ourselves of Jesus' promise in Matthew 28:20: "I'll be with you as you do this, day after day after day, right up to the end of the age." We remember Jesus' death for us *then* and we remember Jesus' presence with us *now*. The Word who moved into the neighborhood two thousand years ago is still living in the neighborhood!

In our preparation for Communion, we offer prayers, sometimes written and sometimes spoken from the heart. I have a personal habit of praying the Jesus Prayer—*Lord Jesus Christ, Son of God, have mercy on me*—before I receive Communion. Prayer is a necessary preparatory step of self-examination and contrition. Prayer is how we draw near to God. Communion is how God draws near to us.

And the name of this sacrament reflects the reality: This sacred practice is called Communion in many Christian traditions because, in the words of Paul, "the cup of blessing which we bless, is it not the *communion* of the blood of Christ? The bread which we break, is it not the *communion* of the body of Christ?" (1 Corinthians 10:16, KJV; emphasis added). Through the bread and the cup, we participate in the very life-giving body and blood of Jesus, and transformation happens!

Take a moment to reflect on the following questions.

1. How often do you celebrate the Lord's Supper? Weekly? Monthly? Quarterly? Sporadically?

2. Can you recall a particularly meaningful time of celebrating the Lord's Supper?

3. In your practice of Communion, do you tend to focus on what Jesus *has done* for us or what he *is doing* now? How could you emphasize the perspective you typically focus on less?

## The Word

Jesus' final meal with his disciples shows us that Christian worship requires human bodies, broken bread, and poured-out wine. Jesus is indeed looking for worshipers who worship God "out of their very being, their spirits, their true selves" (John 4:24), but worship from our spirits must be expressed with our whole selves, whatever that may look like. Worship that remains locked away within our hearts isn't really worship; it's meditation (which is a good and helpful Christian practice). In participating in Communion, we experience a connection between the heavenly and the earthly.

This meal is also the moment when Jesus revealed to his disciples the meaning of his death. The death of Jesus enacted God's promised new covenant, marked by the forgiveness of sins, the end of exile, and the liberation of God's people from sin, Satan, death, fear, hate, and all manner of evil. In *The Day the Revolution Began*, New Testament theologian N. T. Wright writes, "When Jesus wanted to explain to his followers what his forthcoming death was all about, he did not give them a theory, a model, a metaphor, or any other such thing; he gave them a *meal*, a Passover meal."[1]

> On the first of the Days of Unleavened Bread, the disciples came to Jesus and said, "Where do you want us to prepare your Passover meal?"
>
> He said, "Enter the city. Go up to a certain man and say, 'The Teacher says, My time is near. I and my disciples plan to celebrate the Passover meal at your house.'" The disciples followed Jesus' instructions to the letter, and prepared the Passover meal.
>
> MATTHEW 26:17-19

---

Jesus' death was an atoning death in that Jesus took our sins and wiped them out, covering them with his own blood in order to heal and restore us. Yet, surprisingly, Jesus didn't connect his death with the annual Jewish Day of Atonement but instead with the Jewish celebration of Passover, marking God's liberation of the people of God from Egyptian slavery. What's implicit in this connection is that Jesus' death frees us from the power of sin and death in addition to cleansing us from the stain of sin, the result of the sprinkled blood on the Day of Atonement (Leviticus 16:29-31).

> After sunset, he and the Twelve were sitting around the table. During the meal, he said, "I have something hard but important to say to you: One of you is going to hand me over to the conspirators."
>
> They were stunned, and then began to ask, one after another, "It isn't me, is it, Master?"
>
> MATTHEW 26:20-22

---

Jesus had already revealed to his disciples that he was going to be handed over to the chief priests, after which he would be rejected and killed. If that were not shocking enough, then the disciples heard Jesus say that his betrayer would be one of the Twelve. Their jaws dropped as their blood ran cold. They looked at one another with stunned eyes, wondering who would betray their beloved Master.

> Jesus answered, "The one who hands me over is someone I eat with daily, one who passes me food at the table. In one sense the Son of Man is entering into a way of treachery well-marked by the Scriptures—no surprises here. In another sense that man who turns him in, turns traitor to the Son of Man—better never to have been born than do this!"
>
> MATTHEW 26:23-24

---

The Hebrew prophets—particularly Isaiah, as we saw in the previous lesson—noted that Israel's Servant-King would suffer "like a lamb taken to be slaughtered" (Isaiah 53:7). That the Messiah would be mistreated should have been expected, and yet to expect one of Jesus' own disciples to hand him over to the authorities could not have been in the minds of any of them.

> Then Judas, already turned traitor, said, "It isn't me, is it, Rabbi?"
>
> Jesus said, "Don't play games with me, Judas."
>
> MATTHEW 26:25

---

*The Message*'s translation of Jesus' response to Judas captures the mood of the moment. The Greek phrase in Jesus' response is a simple sentence in English: "You said it." In typical Jesus fashion, he did not answer directly, and yet Jesus wasn't merely avoiding Judas's question. What Jesus said communicated his unwillingness to play along with Judas's game of pretending to be innocent. Judas knew. *Jesus knew!* The charade was over. Jesus was done playing games.

During the meal, Jesus took and blessed the bread, broke it, and gave it to his disciples:

> Take, eat.
> This is my body.

MATTHEW 26:26

---

The three movements of Jesus here mark what Jesus does with his church. As Pastor Glenn Packiam notes, we are bread in the hands of Jesus. He takes us, making us his own, and then he *blesses* us, gently *breaks* us open, and *gives* us for the sake of the world.[2] We are the body of Christ broken and given to the world. The Passover bread for Jesus *then* and the Communion bread for us *now* are the body of Jesus. How exactly the bread of Communion is the body of Jesus remains a mystery. Let's keep it mysterious without trying to say too much.

Taking the cup and thanking God, he gave it to them:

> Drink this, all of you.
> This is my blood,
> God's new covenant poured out for many people
> for the forgiveness of sins.

MATTHEW 26:27-28

---

Jesus took the cup and gave thanks to God. "Thanking" is a translation of the Greek word *eucharisteō*, which is where we get *Eucharist*, one of the more traditional names for Communion. When Christians call Communion the Eucharist, they are drawing us back to the Last Supper, where Jesus gave thanks to God before giving the bread and wine to the Twelve. Jesus poured out his blood, his *precious* blood, for the forgiveness of sins—*liberation* from the bondage of sin, *cleansing* of the pollution of sin, and *neutralizing* of the power of sin.

The bread of Communion is Jesus' body broken for us. The cup of wine is Jesus' blood shed for us. Jesus' death, and our subsequent proclamation of his death through Communion, marks the beginning of God's new covenant, a signpost of God's desire to make all things new.

Take a moment to reflect on the following questions.

4. What are the key differences between seeking to understand the meaning of Jesus' death through intellectual speculation and seeking to understand his death by celebrating the Lord's Supper?

5. What do you find significant about Jesus revealing the meaning of his death during the Passover celebration instead of on the Day of Atonement?

6. What would you have felt had you been with Jesus and his disciples at this final meal and heard Jesus say that his betrayer was at the table?

7. If we are bread in Jesus' hands, what does it mean for him to gently break us open?

8. What has been your experience of the blood of Jesus washing away your sin? Think back to a moment when you were aware of liberation from the bondage of sin, cleansing of the pollution of sin, or neutralizing of the power of sin. How did that experience shape you?

## The Neighborhood

We are a Eucharistic people. We are bread in the hands of Jesus. Jesus takes us and blesses us, breaks us open in vulnerability, and gives us to our neighbors, classmates, coworkers, friends, and families. God blesses us not merely *for* us but so that *through* us the blessing of God may extend to others. Jesus moved into the neighborhood, joining us in death to rescue us from death and free us from sin, so we could join him in his work of making things new in our neighborhoods.

9. Have you been resistant to vulnerability, the work of God to break you open? If so, what is keeping you closed off?

10. Who do you need to forgive? Maybe it is a neighbor or coworker. What can you do to move toward forgiveness?

## The Prayer

As you conclude this lesson, offer this prayer.

> *Ever-present God, we thank you for sending Jesus to be our guiding Shepherd and sacrificial Lamb. Thank you for the blood of Jesus. Wash us pure from our sin and set us right. Have mercy on us, forgive us of our sins, and set us free so that we may freely participate in what you are doing in and through us. In Jesus' name, amen.*

LESSON 4

# GOD'S LOVE ON THE LINE

## The Approach

I have accepted the fact that love comes with inherent risks.

We see the undercurrent of those risks in many of our most beloved love stories. Perhaps no love story is more known and cherished than Cinderella, a folktale that has been told and retold in many cultures and in many ways. Like most kids growing up in America, I came to know the Cinderella story through Walt Disney's 1950 animated adaptation, appropriately named *Cinderella*.

The Disney version follows the typical plot: Cinderella is mistreated by her cruel stepmother and her two mean-spirited stepsisters. She lives in an unjust world of forced labor and mockery. She takes respite in unlikely friendship with mice. The king's son is looking for a wife and invites all the eligible women to a royal ball, where the prince will choose his bride. Cinderella wants to attend, but her stepsisters tear her dress apart, and she is left behind in despair.

Her fairy godmother comes to rescue her. She gives Cinderella a beautiful dress and transforms a pumpkin into a lavish carriage and her mice companions into horses. At the ball, Cinderella and the prince meet and share a dance. An instant connection is made, but knowing the magical dress and horse-drawn carriage will disappear at midnight, Cinderella disappears in a rush, leaving one glass slipper behind on the staircase.

The prince, smitten by the mysterious woman he met, wants to marry the owner of the slipper, and a search for her begins. When one of the prince's men arrives at Cinderella's stepmother's home, while Cinderella is locked in the attic, her evil stepsisters are dismayed that the slipper does not fit their feet, and her stepmother causes the glass slipper to be broken. Cinderella is freed by her mice friends and reveals that she has the other glass slipper. When everyone sees it's a perfect fit, she is reunited with the prince, they kiss, and the two of them live, as they say, happily ever after.

As I reflect on that story, I think about the risk involved in this search. There are numerous ways the prince could have found a wife, but after his first dance with Cinderella, his heart had already made the decision. What if he never found her again? Many women from the kingdom had shown up at that ball. What if the search for the perfect foot failed? What if he was rejecting other opportunities for love yet failed to find the woman his heart was set on? What if he found Cinderella after years had passed only to discover that she had married another man? Love sent the prince on a mission, one fraught with inherent risks.

God is familiar with such risks. When God created the world, God filled it with human beings who reflect God's image because God is love. God didn't create people because the Father, Son, and Spirit had grown bored at some point before creation. God willfully chose to create because love is self-giving and by its nature seeks expression. However, in choosing to create beings who would bear the image of God in the world, God knew the risks involved. God created from love and fashioned creatures who would love in turn. But God would not force the creatures made in God's image to love God in return. God would not program them to love against their will. For love to be authentic, love needs to be an unfettered choice. Therein lies the risk.

Much of the Christian life is dependent upon how we respond to the love of God. One constant in the universe is that the God revealed in Jesus is love. God's love never changes. It never shrinks back or turns away. The love of God abides. What fluctuates is human response. If we respond to the love of God with love and devotion, we receive salvation and life with God. If we respond to the love of God with contempt or apathy, we receive condemnation and separation from God, which is not God's desire. God "wants not only us but *everyone* saved, you know, everyone to get to know the truth *we've* learned" (1 Timothy 2:4).

God the Father sent the Son to the world not to condemn the world but that humanity might be saved. And why did God send his one and only Son? Love. Love that risks not receiving love in return. Love that would enter our broken world not with the pointed finger of accusation but with arms spread out on the hard wood of the cross, dying for the sins of the world. John's Gospel puts it this way: "This is how much God loved the world: He gave his Son, his one and only Son. And this is why: so that no one need be destroyed; by believing in him, anyone can have a whole and lasting life" (John 3:16).

Before we move forward, take a moment to reflect on the following questions.

1. If you could go back in time to undo a mistake from your past, what would it be?

2. When have you had to take a risk for an expression of love in your life? What was that experience like?

3. What kind of risk, if any, did God experience in creating human beings?

## The Word

While Jesus reflected on his impending death, offering glimpses into its meaning, the apostles experienced—in real time!—the redeeming work of Jesus' death and, on the other side of the cross and the empty tomb, reflected on the various implications of his death. Writing to the church in Rome, Paul wrote not from a place of detached theological speculation but from a place of embodied understanding. Paul not only knew the theological implications of Jesus' crucifixion—he had experienced a crucifixion of his own, as he testified to the churches of Galatia: "Indeed, I have been crucified with Christ" (Galatians 2:20). Paul had experienced the salvation that he wrote about in his Spirit-inspired letters.

> Christ arrives right on time to make this happen. He didn't, and doesn't, wait for us to get ready. He presented himself for this sacrificial death when we were far too weak and rebellious to do anything to get ourselves ready. And even if we hadn't been so weak, we wouldn't have known what to do anyway.
>
> ROMANS 5:6

What is the "this" that Christ made happen? We have to look back to the opening of Romans 5 to find our answer: "By entering through faith into what God has always wanted to do for us—set us right with him, make us fit for him—we have it all together with God because of our Master Jesus" (Romans 5:1). Through his death we have been *justified*, which *The Message* translates as "set us right with him, make us fit for him." We were created in God's image, made to fit perfectly in a relationship with God—Creator and creature living in harmony. But our sin shattered the image of God in us, so we no longer fit. Weakened by sin, we were without the means to make things right. Twisted by sin, we were too rebellious to even try! Jesus came to us in our rebellion to rescue and redeem us, to set us right with God.

> We can understand someone dying for a person worth dying for, and we can understand how someone good and noble could inspire us to selfless sacrifice.
>
> ROMANS 5:7

---

We all know stories of historic deaths—the soldier diving on a grenade, the firefighter running into a burning building, the unknown bystander who jumps into the water to save a drowning child. These stories of bravery inspire us today just as such stories inspired people in Paul's day. Yet Jesus' death exceeds the nobility of good-person-dying-for-innocent-people stories. Jesus offered himself as a sacrifice for all of us while we were sinning. Jesus offered up himself to make us right with God while we were rebelling.

> But God put his love on the line for us by offering his Son in sacrificial death while we were of no use whatever to him.
>
> ROMANS 5:8

---

The cross represents many things, chief among them the dazzling display of God's love for us and the world. In our brokenness and sin, we haven't courted favor with God, because "we were of no use whatever to him." Humanity hasn't impressed God with our evolving technology, civilized societies, or attempts at moral excellence. In Jesus and through his death, God put his love on the line, risking a once-and-for-all act of redemption. Of course, the risky love of God looks like a risk from our vantage point, but God, who knows all things, knew from the beginning how this rescue plan would work out.

> Now that we are set right with God by means of this sacrificial death, the consummate blood sacrifice, there is no longer a question of being at odds with God in any way.
>
> ROMANS 5:9

---

By trusting the God who puts love on the line, we have been set right with God. The Holy Spirit repairs the image of God within us, which was broken by sin. The blood of Jesus enables us to walk in step with God again. God's work of redemption in us comes with a future hope—that "there is no longer a question of being at odds with God in any way," a helpful rendering of what another English translation describes as being "saved through him from the wrath of God" (Romans 5:9, NRSV). The typical English translation of the Greek word *orgē* as "wrath" is best understood as "judgment" or "condemnation," as seen in the New Living Translation. The translation choice in *The Message* helps us understand that "the wrath of God" implies future judgment—being at odds with God in the age to come. We've been set right with God *now* and we will remain right with God in the future.

> If, when we were at our worst, we were put on friendly terms with God by the sacrificial death of his Son, now that we're at our best, just think of how our lives will expand and deepen by means of his resurrection life! Now that we have actually received this amazing friendship with God, we are no longer content to simply say it in plodding prose. We sing and shout our praises to God through Jesus, the Messiah!
>
> ROMANS 5:10-11

---

In the words of a nineteenth-century hymn: "What a friend we have in Jesus, / all our sins and griefs to bear!"[1] We were in rough shape, broken and enslaved by sin, out of step with the God who made us, but now we have become God's friends. God put everything on the line to come looking for the people of the world so they could experience "real and eternal life, more and better life than they ever dreamed of" (John

10:10). The proper response to the joy we experience through this work of redemption is praise! We sing and shout for joy to the God who made us and rescued us.

Take a moment to reflect on the following questions.

4. Think back to a story of self-sacrifice from literature, film, or the news. What makes that story stand out in your memory?

5. In what ways has the image of God been broken in you? What sins have you been aware of in your own heart and life that have kept you out of step with God?

6. How does sin make us weak?

7. How does it feel to know you have been set right with God now and in the future?

8. What are some creative ways you can express your thanks to God in worship for all that God has done for you and the world?

## The Neighborhood

People in your neighborhood love a good story. We all do! What God has done through Jesus is a story—a love story. It's the best of all love stories, in fact. This true story we call the gospel does more than entertain; the gospel story saves those who believe. We tell and retell the gospel through our acts of worship when we are gathered as the church. But what about with the people in our neighborhoods? Sure, we can and should invite our neighbors to church, but what if they never walk through those doors? As intimidating as it sounds, we have the opportunity to tell them the story of Jesus and his death and resurrection. The best way to tell the gospel story is in the context of our own stories. Don't worry about quoting the right verses of Scripture in sharing the gospel. Rather, tell people what your life was like before Jesus, how you met Jesus, what you learned about what Jesus did for us, and what difference Jesus has made in your life now that you are following him. When we wrap *our experience* of the gospel around the gospel itself, the story of God's love comes alive to people.

9. Is there someone new in your neighborhood you have not met? What is a creative way you could meet them?

10. What would it sound like to sum up your experience of redemption and share it in story form with someone in your neighborhood who is outside the Christian faith?

## The Prayer

As you work on how to tell the gospel story within your story, offer the following prayer.

*Holy Father, thank you for putting your love on the line to save us through the death of Jesus. We were weakened and wrecked by our sin, and now we have been strengthened and restored by the blood of Jesus. May our hearts never grow cold. May the light of the gospel never grow dim. Empower us by your Holy Spirit to be Spirit-inspired storytellers of your goodness and grace. In Jesus' name we pray. Amen.*

LESSON 5

# NO LONGER WANDERING EXILES

## The Approach

I have always wanted to be an insider.

We each have the need for acceptance and a sense of belonging. We all want to go to a place where everyone knows our names. We instinctively keep a careful eye out for our people, our community, where we can know and be known. We're looking for a relational network where we can love and be loved without pretense. Once we find that group of people, we slowly transition from a curious outsider to a cheerful insider. We absorb the values of the community. We learn the language of our people. We follow a similar code of conduct to theirs. We become insiders.

In high school I desperately looked for my people so I wouldn't be such a self-conscious outsider. Sadly, I wasn't athletic enough for the jocks and certainly not smart enough for the academic elites. I was too nerdy for the party crowd and too undisciplined for the marching band. I felt like a social nomad, a foreigner without a homeland. I feared that I would be a permanent outsider. All that changed when I found the church.

I had been baptized as a child, but during middle school I'd drifted from the church. During my sophomore year of high school, I grudgingly made my return. After only a few months of worship, Sunday school, and weekly youth group meetings, I found myself confronted with the gospel. And not only did King Jesus invite me to follow him, but I wouldn't be following him in isolation. In that nondescript church, I found my people.

And for the first time in my life, I felt like an insider.

I suppose the reason I loved the local church then (and why I still love the local church today) is because the people of the church invited me in and pushed out all the social anxiety and insecurity I had felt. They loved me despite my faults, and they loved me through my misdeeds on my way toward growth and transformation. Learning the church lingo proved challenging, but it was a challenge marked by joy.

Once I knew I belonged, I threw myself into the life of the church, particularly on Sunday mornings. I would go to early service, attend Sunday school, and then stay for the second service. My parents questioned why I wanted to attend the same worship service with the same sermon twice. I'd respond enthusiastically with "The sermons are so good. I don't want to miss anything!" I would then return in the late afternoon for youth choir, youth discipleship, and at times the Sunday evening worship services. Sometimes I would even stay afterward to join in the occasional business meetings.

Baptism business meetings were not often populated by teenagers, but I wanted to attend everything because these were my people! I had become an insider, and I wanted to participate in what the people of God were doing in that church.

I remember in one meeting we were voting on a new round of deacons. The meeting leader named each deacon candidate and instructed us to indicate that we were voting for a particular candidate by raising our right hand. The meeting leader said something like "Please indicate your desire to vote for Bob Smith to become a deacon." I immediately shot my hand up into the air, and then, with all sincerity, I looked at the older gentleman sitting next to me and asked, "What's a deacon?"

I'll always appreciate that church for nurturing me in the faith, teaching me to be a Christian insider: someone who follows Jesus, who loves God and people. Their patience with me, in all my youthful exuberance and ignorance, and the values they instilled in me—a devotion to Scripture, a commitment to make disciples, and a love for the church—became ingrained in my heart and laid a foundation that has served me well. I'm thankful that I have been welcomed into the family of God.

Before we move forward, take a moment to reflect on the following questions.

1. Who were your people when you were in high school?

2. What was the first local church you were part of? What did you love about that church? What didn't you love?

3. What insider language, values, or practices have you found the most challenging as a follower of Jesus?

## The Word

As the body of Jesus, the church does in a social way what Jesus does in a spiritual way—that is, turn wandering outsiders into grounded insiders. God's desire from the beginning was to have a big, diverse family. God's sovereign selection of Abraham and his descendants was not so God could have a family of just Jewish insiders. Rather, it would be through Abraham's children that all the families of the earth would be blessed (Genesis 12:3). When Jesus joined us in death through his crucifixion, he "tore down the wall we used to keep each other at a distance" (Ephesians 2:14). He grafted us non-Jewish people into the family of Abraham, creating a new kind of community, a new kind of family.

> Now God has us where he wants us, with all the time in this world and the next to shower grace and kindness upon us in Christ Jesus. Saving is all his idea, and all his work. All we do is trust him enough to let him do it. It's God's gift from start to finish! We don't play the major role. If we did, we'd probably go around bragging that we'd done the whole thing! No, we neither make nor save ourselves. God does both the making and saving. He creates each of us by Christ Jesus to join him in the work he does, the good work he has gotten ready for us to do, work we had better be doing.
>
> EPHESIANS 2:7-10

---

Paul uses the word *saving* (or *salvation*) to describe God's work of rescuing us from the sin that divides us from God, from one another, and from our true selves. God has chosen to save the world through us and with us, but make no mistake—saving is what God does. God created us, knitting us together in our mothers' wombs, and in saving us, God is *recreating* us to look like Jesus. We participate by receiving this work with gratitude, and then we lace up our boots and go to work with Jesus in recreating the entire world.

> But don't take any of this for granted. It was only yesterday that you outsiders to God's ways had no idea of any of this, didn't know the first thing about the

> way God works, hadn't the faintest idea of Christ. You knew nothing of that rich history of God's covenants and promises in Israel, hadn't a clue about what God was doing in the world at large. Now because of Christ—dying that death, shedding that blood—you who were once out of it altogether are in on everything.
>
> EPHESIANS 2:11-13

---

In ancient Jewish worship, the high priest would enter the innermost part of the Temple and there would sprinkle blood on the mercy seat, the lid to the Ark of the Covenant. This sacred act occurred one time a year, on the Day of Atonement. This act cleansed the people of Israel of their sins (Leviticus 16:30). Non-Jewish people had no knowledge of God's work of atonement and had experienced none of its saving benefits until Jesus came. His atoning death brought outsiders from the pagan outskirts of town to the very heart of God's covenant city.

> The Messiah has made things up between us so that we're now together on this, both non-Jewish outsiders and Jewish insiders. He tore down the wall we used to keep each other at a distance. He repealed the law code that had become so clogged with fine print and footnotes that it hindered more than it helped. Then he started over. Instead of continuing with two groups of people separated by centuries of animosity and suspicion, he created a new kind of human being, a fresh start for everybody.
>
> EPHESIANS 2:14-15

---

Jesus' death with us and for us "broke down the wall of hostility that separated us" (Ephesians 2:14, NLT). Walls of racism and hate, walls determined by socioeconomic status and educational level, and walls of political and religious divisions came crashing down through Jesus' crucifixion and death. In cleansing us of our sins, Jesus not only restored our relationship with God but also opened the door to restored relationships with one another. The dream of a true kinship of all humankind was made possible through Jesus' death. In fact, those who follow Jesus through faith and baptism have become a new people, a new humanity marked not by hostility and division but by goodwill and unity.

> Christ brought us together through his death on the cross. The Cross got us to embrace, and that was the end of the hostility. Christ came and preached peace to you outsiders and peace to us insiders. He treated us as equals, and so made us equals. Through him we both share the same Spirit and have equal access to the Father.
>
> EPHESIANS 2:16-18

---

Jesus wiped away the hostility that kept outsiders from experiencing the peace and joy of belonging. Jesus came with a message of peace to both Jewish and non-Jewish people. It's worth noting that it was a message of peace to those who accepted. Using provocative language, Jesus did say on one occasion, "Don't imagine that I came to bring peace to the earth! I came not to bring peace, but a sword" (Matthew 10:34, NLT). The sword Jesus was talking about was the inevitable sword of division when people who reject his gospel message divide themselves from those who accept the gospel. Those who believe in Jesus receive his gospel as peace and redemption. Those who reject it experience the gospel as exclusionary and condemning.

> That's plain enough, isn't it? You're no longer wandering exiles. This kingdom of faith is now your home country. You're no longer strangers or outsiders. You *belong* here, with as much right to the name Christian as anyone. God is building a home. He's using us all—irrespective of how we got here—in what he is building. He used the apostles and prophets for the foundation. Now he's using you, fitting you in brick by brick, stone by stone, with Christ Jesus as the cornerstone that holds all the parts together. We see it taking shape day after day—a holy temple built by God, all of us built into it, a temple in which God is quite at home.
>
> EPHESIANS 2:19-22

---

The Temple where the sacred Day of Atonement was celebrated has now been reimagined in light of Jesus' life, death, resurrection, and ascension. God's constructing a new temple using me and you. We have been rescued by Jesus joining us in death, and God has brought us into the family of God. In Jesus, we experience the acceptance and sense of belonging we have all longed for.

Reflect on the following questions.

4. How have you experienced salvation as an end to separation from God, other people, or your true self?

5. If salvation is God's work and gift "from start to finish" (Ephesians 2:8), then what does it look like for us to participate in God's work?

6. Why is sin something we need to be cleansed from?

7. What are the biggest walls of division and hostility you see in your corner of the world?

8. How does it feel to know you are not an outsider but a beloved insider, safe and secure in the family of God?

## The Neighborhood

Who do you know at work or at school or in your neighborhood who seems isolated and alone? Maybe they have chosen to make themselves an outsider. Maybe not. Perhaps they are shy or introverted and prefer to be on their own. Perhaps not.

Jesus, the Word of God, moved into the neighborhood and joined us in real human death to rescue us from sin and experiences like isolation, loneliness, and feeling abandoned. Reaching out with a simple text or a friendly hello to someone who seems like a stranger could be the first step toward their acceptance of the gospel.

9. What are the obstacles toward reaching out to outsiders in your neighborhood? Busyness? Fear? Lack of knowing how to connect with a stranger? Note the biggest obstacle and pray about it openly and honestly.

10. What practical steps can you take to reach out to those who seem like outsiders?

## The Prayer

With your attention on your neighborhood, offer this following prayer.

*God of all grace, you have invited us into your family through Jesus Christ. Through your loving act of redemption, we have found ourselves welcomed into this new temple you are building. May the walls of hostility and division continue to fall in our neighborhoods as we work for the things that make for peace. In Jesus' name we pray. Amen.*

LESSON 6

# A PERFECT PRIEST, A PERFECT SACRIFICE

## The Approach

I've never been perfect at anything anywhere at any time in my life.

Growing up I constantly looked for one thing that I could master, where I could say, "I am really, really good at this!" I never found that one thing. My life has been a long series of blunders, miscalculations, missteps, and mistakes. Today I still find myself working to hone my craft as a pastor, preacher, teacher, and writer. Perhaps growing and improving, striving toward the elusive ideal of perfection, is a shared human experience. We all struggle and strive. None of us was born as a master at any one thing.

In the Sermon on the Mount, just after Jesus taught us to love our enemies, challenging us not just to love those who love us, he said in emphatic terms, "You are to be perfect, even as your Father in heaven is perfect" (Matthew 5:48, NLT). The Greek word translated "perfect" in this verse finds its root in the word *telos*, meaning "fulfillment" or "reaching the designed end or termination point." *Telos* doesn't mean "perfection" in terms of error-free flawlessness. This kind of perfection could be rendered "maturity" or "fully developed." *The Message* translates Jesus' exhortation as "*Grow up*. You're kingdom subjects. Now live like it. Live out your God-created identity" (Matthew 5:48).

Perfectionism, with its fear of failure and penchant toward faultfinding and pessimism, lacks the adequate power or motivation to help us grow up. Perfectionism inevitably leads to legalism, which will sooner or later lead to hypocrisy. Jesus saved his greatest critique and sharpest words for two kinds of people—those who harm children (Matthew 18:6-7) and those who practice religious hypocrisy (Matthew 23). Legalism is a shortcut attempt at Christian maturity rooted in behavior modification that skips the hard work of character formation. When we only focus on behaviors, the temptation to fill the role of a playactor on the stage of life becomes too great.

I have caught myself auditioning for that role plenty of times. When my wife and I were first married, I had a bad habit of practicing a pretend spirituality. We were married in our early twenties, and we spent our first couple of years together figuring out life while I was in college and seminary. I wanted to be a good husband, but more than that, I wanted her to know that I was serious in my pursuit of God, who had called me into vocational ministry. On the days when I didn't carve out time for prayer and Bible reading, I would leave my Bible open on the coffee table so that when she woke up and walked into the living room she would think I had read my Bible that morning. I doubt she even noticed. But when I came to my senses, I repented. I confessed my sin to her, even though she was unaware of it, and I took a moment in prayer to confess this sin to God, too.

Consider me a recovering hypocrite.

Jesus wants us to grow up like God is "grown up." Jesus wants us to be fully developed men and women who reflect the image of God. Becoming image bearers who reflect the nature of the God who created us is our *telos*, the goal common to all humanity. Since God, who is Father, Son, and Holy Spirit, is love, we move toward maturity as we grow in the practice of love. To be perfect is to love well, and while Jesus is the only one among us to have done so, his perfect sacrifice for us enables us to grow in the direction of perfect love.

Before we move forward, take a moment to reflect on the following questions.

1. Do you consider yourself a master—that is, more than proficient—at any one thing?

2. Has there been a time in your life when you've been tempted by hypocrisy?

3. What does it look like to grow in the practice of love?

## The Word

I have a devotional habit of drawing a cross in the margin of my Bible when I come across a passage that mentions the death of Jesus or draws out the implications of Jesus' death. No book of the Bible has more crosses in the margin than Hebrews. Understanding the meaning of Jesus' death requires grounding our interpretations in a biblical—specifically an Old Testament—context. The many references to Jesus' death in Hebrews mean what they mean when read from a Jewish point of view. Jesus died as our Jewish High Priest, summing up the Jewish sacrificial system in his death. Below are a few references to Jesus' death in Hebrews:

- "He also bypassed the sacrifices consisting of goat and calf blood, instead using his own blood as the price to set us free once and for all. . . . Think how much more the blood of Christ cleans up our whole lives, inside and out. Through the Spirit, Christ offered himself as an unblemished sacrifice" (Hebrews 9:12, 14-15).
- "Christ didn't enter the earthly version of the Holy Place; he entered the Place Itself, and offered himself to God as the sacrifice for our sins" (Hebrews 9:24).
- "He set aside the first in order to enact the new plan—*God's* way—by which we are made fit for God by the once-for-all sacrifice of Jesus" (Hebrews 10:9-10).
- "He was crucified outside the city gates—*that* is where he poured out the sacrificial blood that was brought to God's altar to cleanse his people" (Hebrews 13:12).

Hebrews offers us a treasure trove of Jewish images and ideas to see the beauty of Jesus' death on our behalf.

The single act of Jesus joining us in death on the cross remains the centerpiece of our faith. As we saw in an earlier lesson, the high priest would go into the Holy of Holies one time a year, on the Day of Atonement, and offer the blood of a sacrificed animal. Jesus shed his blood as the sacrificial Lamb, and he offered his blood as our High Priest. According to Leviticus, "on this day atonement will be made for you, to cleanse you. In the presence of God you will be made clean of all your sins" (Leviticus 16:30). This act of atonement—Jesus' sacrificial death on the cross—purified God's people from the pollutant of sin.

> So now we have a high priest who perfectly fits our needs: completely holy, uncompromised by sin, with authority extending as high as God's presence in heaven itself.
>
> HEBREWS 7:26

Jesus moved into our neighborhood looking like one of us. He was human in every way except one: He was perfected in love right from the beginning, so even though he was tempted by sin, Jesus was not corrupted by sin. Therefore, he was the perfect High Priest, the perfect fit for what we needed—someone to take away our sin!

> Unlike the other high priests, he doesn't have to offer sacrifices for his own sins every day before he can get around to us and our sins. He's done it, once and for all: offered up *himself* as the sacrifice.
>
> HEBREWS 7:27

As laid out in the Levitical law, on the Day of Atonement the high priest had to first sacrifice a bull to make atonement for himself (Leviticus 16:11-14). The priest wasn't perfect and therefore had to be cleansed of his sins before offering atonement for the sins of the rest of God's people. Jesus, who was without sin, had no need to make atonement for himself. He came to his people as the perfect sacrifice.

> The law appoints as high priests men who are never able to get the job done right. But this intervening command of God, which came later, appoints the Son, who is absolutely, eternally perfect.
>
> HEBREWS 7:28

While necessary and helpful, the high priest, as an example to the rest of the ancient people of God under the old covenant, was not able to get the job done in a lasting way. We read the story of Israel as one of victory *and defeat*, faithfulness *and compromise*, righteousness *and sinfulness*. God loved Israel, who bore the mark of the covenant but did not remain faithful to that covenant.

> Every priest goes to work at the altar each day, offers the same old sacrifices year in, year out, and never makes a dent in the sin problem.
>
> HEBREWS 10:11

While the annual Day of Atonement offered some remedy to the destructive nature of sin, it did very little to solve the problem of Israel's repetitive cycle of faithfulness, idolatry, judgment, and then a return to faithfulness. Israel's sin problem wasn't only that they were ceremonially unclean but that their heart dispositions remained crooked, slanted toward the idolatry and injustice God continued to warn them about.

> As a priest, Christ made a single sacrifice for sins, and that was it! Then he sat down right beside God and waited for his enemies to cave in.
>
> HEBREWS 10:12-13

Jesus joined humanity in death, offering his life as a sacrifice for the sin of all people—both Jew and Gentile. As Paul emphatically claims, whether we are Jewish insiders or Gentile outsiders, we all "start out in identical conditions, which is to say that we all start out as sinners" (Romans 3:9). All humanity needs to be rescued from the enemies that are sin, death, hell, and evil. The fortresses built by these enemies came crashing down by the power of Jesus' death.

> It was a perfect sacrifice by a perfect person to perfect some very imperfect people. By that single offering, he did everything that needed to be done for everyone who takes part in the purifying process.
>
> HEBREWS 10:14

None of us master the art of living as human beings fully alive. None of us are *perfect*, but we are *being perfected*. Jesus, the perfect Priest, offered the perfect sacrifice to rescue us and perfect us in love. We have been rescued, yes, but we are also *being* rescued. The sacrifice of Jesus' own life continues to purify us from the pollutant of sin just as the blood of goats purified ancient Israel, though his sacrifice was "once-for-all" (Hebrews 10:10). The effects of redemption in our lives come slowly.

Take a moment to reflect on the following questions.

4. Where in the Old Testament do we see the cycle of faithfulness, idolatry, judgment, and a return to faithfulness?

5. If you were a Jewish high priest commissioned with offering sacrifices on the Day of Atonement, how would you have felt as you walked into the Holy of Holies to offer blood on the mercy seat?

6. Why was the Day of Atonement inadequate to prevent Israel from drifting into idolatry and injustice?

7. What makes our shared enemies—sin, death, hell, and evil—such villains in the story God is writing in our lives?

8. What does it look like for the work of redemption in our lives to be a process and not just a one-time event?

## The Neighborhood

The perfect neighborhood would be a place where people know each other, watch out for one another, and advocate for one another. Sadly, nobody lives in a perfect neighborhood; however, we do have the opportunity to grow up and become mature in our neighborliness. Jesus died to set us free—and for what? In his letter to the Galatians, Paul reminds us not to use our freedom for self-indulgence: "It is absolutely clear that God has called you to a free life. Just make sure that you don't use this freedom as an excuse to do whatever you want to do and destroy your freedom. Rather, use your freedom to serve one another in love; that's how freedom grows" (Galatians 5:13).

9. Who can you serve in your neighborhood, and what can you do to serve them?

10. How can you use your freedom in the way God intends?

## The Prayer

With your mind on who you can serve in your neighborhood, offer the following prayer.

---

> *Lord Jesus, our perfect High Priest, you offered yourself as a perfect sacrifice for us. We are very aware of our imperfections and humbly ask that you perfect us in love. Thank you for breathing life into us and for the gift of a new life through your sacrifice. Show us how we can serve those around us for the glory of your name. Amen.*

LESSON 7

# HIS WOUNDS, OUR HEALING

## The Approach

I have never broken a bone in my body—*at least not yet!*

I tense up anytime I hear reports of a professional football player with a season-ending broken leg or ankle. Obviously I hope I never experience a bone break (or any catastrophic injury, for that matter). Breaks, I have had none, but wounds, I have had plenty. Both flesh wounds and heart wounds have found their way into my life over the years.

While I was a seminary student, I was cutting index cards in half in my apartment to create flash cards for my Introduction to New Testament Greek class. I would have asked my wife to cut the cards (she has always been better with scissors than me), but she was out of town. I was holding a large stack (too large of a stack!) of index cards with my left hand and squeezing the scissors hard (too hard!) with my right hand. Foolishly, my eyes didn't see where the tips of the scissors were going to come together once the cards were completely cut. With one final squeeze, I snipped a half-inch gash in my hand with the tip of those sharp scissors. I immediately stood up, knowing the seriousness of the injury. I grabbed a stack of paper napkins near me and applied direct pressure. I slowly walked to the bathroom to assess the severity of the cut, and as soon as I removed the napkins, blood flowed down my hand and into the sink.

I tied my napkin bandage to my hand with a bandana and drove to our local ER. As the doctor stitched me up—five stitches in all—I told him that I was a seminary student and my wife was out of town for the weekend. He smirked and said, "She left you unattended for a day, and look what happened!" We both laughed. The wound hurt, especially when the localized anesthesia wore off, but the kindness and humor of that ER doctor brought healing in more ways than one.

As a pastor, I'm often in places where wounds are made known—relational wounds, addiction wounds, social wounds, mental-health wounds, and at times, physical wounds. Human beings are frail, delicate creatures. Even though it's difficult, I refuse to let my heart become calloused by all the ways we hurt each other.

I'm most concerned with the wounds we carry but never reveal. I think about veterans who carry the wounds of war in their bodies and souls. I lament the foolishness in thinking dropping bombs on those we label enemies will accomplish anything more than multiplying enemies. I weep for the lives lost. I weep for those who have seen combat and bear wounds that we never see.

Woundedness weakens us, whether the hurt we experience occurs on the battlefield or in the boardroom, and we spend too much energy and effort covering up the things that make us feel weak. We don't want anyone to see our weaknesses, at least not in a culture that rewards strength. We live at a time when unmatched strength and unblemished beauty draw praise, even when such strength is an act and the appearance of beauty is digitally enhanced. We believe that any sign of brokenness or damage must be buried if we are to find love and acceptance. We mask all those tiny little wounds in our humanity because we fear the shame we may feel when people see the damage stacked up in our souls. Sadly, such posturing and pretending only makes our condition worse. Our inattention to our woundedness only deepens the wounds.

The good news is that we no longer have to hide. King Jesus has entered suffering humanity and borne our wounds publicly in the brightness of the morning sun! When he moved into the neighborhood, he did not come to show the prosperous how to gain more; he came to show the broken how to become whole through his grace. Nobody makes it through life unscarred, but Jesus' wounds provide the healing for all that ails us. In Adam, we are all wounded. In Jesus, we are all healed. Do you believe this?

Without faith, the wounds of Jesus appear to be a waste—a wasted life, wasted sorrow, wasted blood. From his sacred hands, feet, and side, blood flowed and spilled on the ground to be trampled upon. His cross was stained red like so many Roman crosses of the first century. To the eyes of the uninitiated and unbelieving bystanders, the execution of Jesus produced a sad ending to a life cut short. But God's grace directs Jesus' blood toward the pain of humanity, and by faith, we humbly receive his blood, which heals us in body and soul.

Before we move forward, take a moment to reflect on the following questions.

1. What is the worst physical injury you have sustained?

2. Do you believe God heals our bodies today, or do you believe miracles of healing ended with the ministry of the apostles?

3. Why do we try to hide our woundedness?

## The Word

Jesus' descent into hell, into the abode of the dead, remains one of the most debated mysteries of the faith. In the words of the Apostles' Creed, we confess that "he descended to the dead."[1] Some traditions use the word *hell* in place of "the dead." The word *hell* is used in the Athanasian Creed: "Christ . . . suffered for our salvation, descended into hell . . ."[2] So what was Jesus doing in hell—that is, the place of the dead? The apostle Peter gives us some indication in his first letter:

> That's what Christ did definitively: suffered because of others' sins, the Righteous One for the unrighteous ones. He went through it all—was put to death and then made alive—to bring us to God.
>
> He went and proclaimed God's salvation to earlier generations who ended up in the prison of judgment because they wouldn't listen.
>
> 1 PETER 3:18-20

Jesus suffered with us on the cross. His suffering ended there. He descended into the abode of the dead to liberate those who were there. Jesus first descended from heaven to earth to join us in our humanity—he moved into the neighborhood. Then he descended from humanity to *suffering* humanity. Finally, Jesus descended as far down as he could go—into death, real human death—as our representative.

This death did not separate him from God his Father because the Father and Son are forever and permanently one.[3]

His soul descended as his body lay in a borrowed tomb. But Jesus would not stay there long. On the third day he rose from the dead! The resurrection was the first step of Jesus' ascension. He did not ascend into resurrection life without first descending into suffering humanity through his crucifixion and death.

Paradoxically, Jesus' suffering became our blessing; his wounds became our healing. Jesus moved into the neighborhood as a healer in fulfillment of Isaiah's prophecy:

> He relieved the inwardly tormented. He cured the bodily ill. He fulfilled Isaiah's well-known revelation:
>
> He took our illnesses,
> He carried our diseases.
>
> MATTHEW 8:16-17

Jesus' healing ministry, culminating in his sacrificial death, shows us how to walk down the road that is marked with suffering but leads to healing.

> This is the kind of life you've been invited into, the kind of life Christ lived. He suffered everything that came his way so you would know that it could be done, and also know how to do it, step-by-step.
>
> 1 PETER 2:21

Jesus joined us in life to show us how to live. His life not only saves us from death but also demonstrates how to live as human beings fully alive. The cross both rescues and reveals. Jesus is our Savior. His once-for-all death wipes out our sins and breaks the power sin and death held over us. We trust in this atoning work done for us. His death also shows us that an authentic human life cannot avoid suffering. If we are going to walk in the footsteps of Jesus, we must acknowledge that suffering will come our way. But with Jesus as our example and guide, we know how to deal with suffering when it arrives.

> He never did one thing wrong,
> Not once said anything amiss.
> 1 PETER 2:22

Though Jesus suffered, he never sinned in word or deed. Peter drew these lines from Isaiah 53:9, which is clear when Peter's words (in their original language, Greek) are compared with the Greek translation of Isaiah 53. As emphasized by Matthew and many of the other New Testament writers, Jesus' life, death, and resurrection came as a direct fulfillment of the Old Testament Law and Prophets. In fact, it seems as if the New Testament writers combed through the Old Testament looking for Jesus in every word and image.

> They called him every name in the book and he said nothing back. He suffered in silence, content to let God set things right.
> 1 PETER 2:23

At his trial, Jesus said very little. Even when he was sentenced to death, he remained silent. When his accusers mocked him, spat upon him, and slapped him, Jesus didn't respond. In all his unjust treatment, Jesus refused to lash out with words of retribution. He refused to defend his innocence. He suffered the indignity of others' mistreatment because he trusted in God's judgment, an idea *The Message* translates as saying that Jesus was "content to let God set things right." While acts of human punishment may be part of God's judgment, the goal has always been to set things right.

> He used his servant body to carry our sins to the Cross so we could be rid of sin, free to live the right way. His wounds became your healing.
> 1 PETER 2:24

Describing exactly *how* the death of Jesus saves us from sin has been a topic of debate among theologians for centuries, but one thing is clear—Jesus' death takes away our sin. We believe the testimony of John the Baptizer, who said, "Look! The Lamb of God who takes away the sin of the world!" (John 1:29, NLT). We are free from sin and ready to live the way God intended, not weighed down and hampered by our brokenness. Jesus' wounds became healing for us.

> You were lost sheep with no idea who you were or where you were going. Now you're named and kept for good by the Shepherd of your souls.
>
> 1 PETER 2:25

Before Jesus' death, we were enslaved by sin and not sure which direction to go. We were sick and lost. Jesus moved into our neighborhood as our Savior and Shepherd, to save us and lead us into God's Kingdom, where God is making all things new.

Take a moment to reflect on the following questions.

4. Pause for a little while and think about the reality of suffering as a follower of Jesus. How does that make you feel?

5. From what does the cross rescue us? What does the cross reveal to us?

6. What do you find remarkable about Jesus' silence during his suffering?

7. What are some theories or metaphors you have heard people use to describe how the death of Jesus saves us from sin?

8. In which area of your life do you need healing today? Your body? Your mind? Your relationships? Your heart?

## The Neighborhood

As we get to know our neighbors, it doesn't take long for us to see their woundedness or for them to see ours if we are willing to unmask it. It's rare for people to live their authentic lives right out in the open because many of us are intentionally private. I never want to pry into my neighbors' lives by asking the wrong question at the wrong time. But I do want to be open with my neighbors. I want my compassion to spill over into friendly neighborliness enough that they feel comfortable sharing their struggles and woundedness with me. It's not that I'll always be able to bring the cure, but I can offer prayer or a hug or sometimes just enough time to listen. Jesus is my Healer and their Healer. As a member of Jesus' body, I can be an extension of his healing to neighbors in need.

9. What do you do to make yourself available to neighbors in need?

10. How can you respond the next time a neighbor opens up and shares a personal struggle with you?

## The Prayer

As you reflect on your woundedness and the wounds of your neighbors, offer the following prayer.

*God of all grace, we are a beat-up and wounded people. We need your help. We need your intervention. We need your healing power to be known among us. Thank you for the gift of your Son, our Savior, Jesus Christ. We believe that his wounded body has become our healing grace. Multiply that healing among us so that we may be whole—body and soul. For the honor of your name, amen.*

LESSON 8

# A DEATH THAT TRIGGERED LIFE

## The Approach

I have never been one to stress over or obsess about money—at least most of the time.

When I was sixteen years old, I shared with my parents my desire to serve in full-time vocational ministry. Most teenagers don't know what they want for dinner, let alone what they want to do with the rest of their lives. But I was confident that God had met me in prayer and given me a distinct and definite call to service in the local church. I wanted to be a pastor.

My parents were supportive, but my mom wisely wanted to test my resolve. She went to our local church and obtained a copy of the church budget. She circled the salary of each pastor and handed the stack of carefully stapled papers to me. She said, "Look at these salaries. Are you sure you want to be a pastor?" Her loving pushback helped me wrestle seriously with such a big decision.

These days, whenever young adults ask about my life as a pastor and then share that they are discerning whether to enter vocational ministry, I typically ask, "Is there anything else you can do? Can you imagine yourself doing something else? Is there a different career path that you can envision making you truly happy? If so, go do that." I offer this challenge not to be discouraging but, much like my mom, because I want to help them wrestle with the authenticity of the call.

As a teenager, the expectation of a relatively low salary didn't deter me. When I was a young adult, I couldn't imagine doing anything other than serving as a pastor. I still can't. I'm not a pastor for the acclaim, and I'm certainly not in it for the money. It's a calling for me. All these years later, this call from God still feels like fire shut up in my bones.

While I have been tempted by a great deal of things—power, pride, selfish ambition, and the like—I haven't been tempted by greed for more. I have generally been content with what I have. (*Except for books! One cannot have too many of those.*) Our consumerist impulses driven by a free-market economy trick us into believing that having more possessions will make us feel happier. Most of the time I have resisted that impulse.

Jesus said, "Take care! Protect yourself against the least bit of greed. Life is not defined by what you have, even when you have a lot" (Luke 12:15). We seem to know instinctively that having more and more things will not necessarily make us happy. Yet we continue to strive for more. The truth is, the more *stuff* we have, the more *stress* we have. Granted, we do need some possessions. We each need a place to live, things to wear, a way to get around, and food to eat. Greed makes us dissatisfied with what we have and mesmerizes us with the one-word mantra of capitalism—"More."

While Jesus warned us that life isn't defined by what we have, many of us have bought into the mantra of "More." We assume we can find the elusive "good life" in a sea of wealth and mountains of possessions. Jesus wants us to experience life—full, unfiltered life—but that life is not one marked by how much we have. Jesus said, "A thief is only there to steal and kill and destroy. I came so they can have real and eternal life, more and better life than they ever dreamed of" (John 10:10). This kind of life is not a life of luxury but one of love; it's marked not by self-satisfying gain but by self-sacrificial giving.

God has put a desire within each of us for the good life, a satisfying and fulfilling life where things go well for us. We all long for what the ancient Greeks called *eudaimonia*, meaning "happiness" or "human flourishing," and what the ancient Jews called *shalom*, meaning "peace." Since we were created in the image of God, this "real and eternal life" is shaped by the God who created us. Without union with God, we become disassociated from our identity as image bearers of God. Sin damages but does not remove that image. When separated from God, we live with that image broken within us. The good life—the "real and eternal life" Jesus speaks of—begins with an active life with God; through God's neighboring presence with us, the Holy Spirit works to restore that image. The Christian view of the good life starts with our eyes looking toward heaven, our feet planted firmly on the teachings of Jesus, and our lungs filled with the breath of life, the Holy Spirit.

In the Old Testament, the prophet Micah describes the good life offered to us in Jesus in simple terms: "The LORD has told you what is good, / and this is what he requires of you: / to do what is right, to love mercy, / and to walk humbly with your God" (Micah 6:8, NLT). The good life, made possible by Jesus' sacrificial death, is a life exemplified by doing what is right, loving mercy, and walking humbly with God. These three exhortations are enough to displace the privileged position pride, greed, and self-absorption have taken in our church.

- *Do what is right.*
- *Love mercy.*
- *Walk humbly with God.*

These three exhortations offer a pathway toward the life Jesus wants for us.

In view of the good life God has for us, reflect on the following questions.

1. What is the one thing you really wanted as a child that you thought would make you happy forever?

2. What do you think about the statement "The more *stuff* we have, the more *stress* we have"? Have you found this to be true?

3. Which of the three exhortations found in Micah 6:8 do you think is the most challenging for Christians today?

## The Word

In John's Gospel, we encounter the Word, who took on flesh and "moved into the neighborhood" (John 1:14). John describes the Word of God as the means by which creation came into existence. According to John,

> Everything was created through him;
> nothing—not one thing!—
> came into being without him.

> What came into existence was Life,
> and the Life was Light to live by.
> The Life-Light blazed out of the darkness;
> the darkness couldn't put it out.
>
> JOHN 1:3-5

Biblical writers, like John, love to play with metaphors of light and dark. Through Jesus, the living Word of God, God created life shining with the brilliance of a summer sunrise, a brightness that no darkness could tamp down or put out.

Later in his Gospel, John reveals that Jesus himself embodies this blazing "Life-Light." Jesus addresses a crowd at the Temple, saying, "I am the world's Light. No one who follows me stumbles around in the darkness. I provide plenty of light to live in" (John 8:12). He offers them an illuminated path out of the darkness of ignorance and sin, a path that will lead them to the good life they so desperately desire.

In his first letter to the Thessalonians, Paul employs a similar contrast between light and dark:

> Friends, you're not in the dark, so how could you be taken off guard by any of this? You're sons of Light, daughters of Day. We live under wide open skies and know where we stand.
>
> 1 THESSALONIANS 5:4-5

By his blood, Jesus purchased us who were enslaved to sin. Jesus set us free from our captivity, delivering us "out of the darkness into his wonderful light" (1 Peter 2:9, NLT). Experiencing this liberation changed our identity. We are no longer sons and daughters of darkness but "sons of Light" and "daughters of Day." Our season of stumbling around in the dark, trying in vain to cobble together a life on our own, is over. We now stand in the light of God's love.

> So let's not sleepwalk through life like those others. Let's keep our eyes open and be smart. People sleep at night and get drunk at night. But not us!
>
> 1 THESSALONIANS 5:6-8

---

As Kingdom citizens, we are fully awake. Jesus didn't rescue us simply to take us to heaven when we die but also to make us the vehicle by which heaven floods the earth. We do not walk like our sleepy and drunken neighbors do. We walk and live according to the values of the Kingdom of God. In Ephesians, Paul contrasts the cheap escape found in drinking in excess to the life we experience in the Spirit: "Don't drink too much wine. That cheapens your life. Drink the Spirit of God, huge drafts of him" (Ephesians 5:18). We don't live our lives under the intoxicating influence of wine. Rather, we live under the intoxicating influence of the Spirit, who is at work making us look more like Jesus.

> Since we're creatures of Day, let's act like it. Walk out into the daylight sober, dressed up in faith, love, and the hope of salvation.
>
> 1 THESSALONIANS 5:8

---

We walk differently than those who are sleepwalking through the world. We also dress differently than they do. Instead of wearing cynicism, despair, and hate, we are dressed up in faith, hope, and love. Thomas Aquinas called these three essential virtues—faith, hope, and love—theological virtues because they were given to us by God to form and shape our character.[1] Paul commonly clusters them together, most memorably in 1 Corinthians 13:13: "Three things will last forever—faith, hope, and love—and the greatest of these is love" (NLT).

> God didn't set us up for an angry rejection but for salvation by our Master, Jesus Christ.
>
> 1 THESSALONIANS 5:9

---

As we have seen, the typical English translation of *orgē* as "wrath" in places like Romans 5:9 is best understood in terms of God's future pending judgment. God created us for life, not death; for covenant, not condemnation; for redemption, not rejection. Jesus joins us in death to defeat death so that we won't experience any kind of angry rejection from God. From the beginning, God never intended to reject us but to save us through Jesus.

> He died for us, a death that triggered life. Whether we're awake with the living or asleep with the dead, we're *alive* with him!
>
> 1 THESSALONIANS 5:10

---

Jesus died with us and for us. He did not die for himself. He died on our behalf, as our human representative. While other human deaths produce little more than inspiration, the death of Jesus triggered life! The same life created by God in the beginning has been recreated through the death of Jesus. We no longer fear death because—whether walking around with the living or asleep, waiting for bodily resurrection—we are alive in Jesus! "Everyone who lives believing in me," Jesus said to Martha of Bethany, "does not ultimately die at all" (John 11:26).

Take a moment to reflect on the following questions.

4. What emotions come to the surface of your heart when you meditate on the contrast between the darkness of the world and the light of Jesus? What makes literal darkness so ominous and literal light so joyful?

5. How did your life change once you came into the light of God's love?

6. How can we live under the intoxicating influence of the Spirit?

7. What does it look like to have your character shaped by the faith, hope, and love given to you by God?

8. How do we as followers of Jesus face our own impending deaths with hope?

## The Neighborhood

What do you wear around your neighborhood? Hopefully the culture of your neighborhood doesn't require formal attire. Can you wear your pajamas and bathrobe outside your house and around your neighborhood? Perhaps you can, but maybe a better question is whether you should! Regardless of your literal attire, God is much more concerned with your metaphorical attire—that is, your attitude. What kind of attitude are you dressed in when you are out and about in your neighborhood? Does it reflect an attitude of death or an attitude of life? An attitude of despair or an attitude of hope?

9. What would it look like for you to be dressed in faith, hope, and love in your neighborhood?

10. What is one small attitude adjustment you could make to change the climate of your neighborhood?

## The Prayer

As you reflect on the new life you are experiencing in Jesus, a life triggered by his death, offer the following prayer.

*Lord Jesus, you are our anchor of hope and the rock of our salvation. Thank you for your precious death, which has given us new life. We humbly ask that you guide us as we serve the people in our neighborhoods. May we be properly dressed in faith, hope, and love so that people may see our good work and praise not us but you. For your name's sake, amen.*

# AS WE GO

A study of the crucifixion of Jesus humbles me and leads me to a place of praise. I believe in the value of Bible study—learning from Holy Scripture, wrestling with theology, and growing in our faith. Jesus commands us to love God with *all our minds* not simply because intellectual pursuits make us smarter but because growing in the knowledge of God naturally leads us to bow our hearts in worship. *Theology leads to doxology.*

As the apostle Paul wraps up his letter to the Romans, he punctuates all he has had to say about the work of God in Jesus (including Jesus' sacrificial death) with praise for the generosity and wisdom of God:

> Have you ever come on anything quite like this extravagant generosity of God, this deep, deep wisdom? It's way over our heads. We'll never figure it out.
>
> Is there anyone around who can explain God?
> Anyone smart enough to tell him what to do?
> Anyone who has done him such a huge favor
> that God has to ask his advice?
>
> Everything comes from him;
> Everything happens through him;

> Everything ends up in him.
> Always glory! Always praise!
>     Yes. Yes. Yes.
>
> ROMANS 11:33-36

---

You don't need to understand every dimension and detail of the meaning of the crucifixion to bow your head, lift up your hands, and thank God for the beauty and the power of the cross. I've been studying, writing about, and teaching on the meaning of Jesus' death for over twenty-five years, and I've yet to answer every question. The good news is that we're not saved by our understanding of the death of Jesus—we are saved by God *through* the death of Jesus. I have yet to reach the bottom of exploring how the crucifixion of one man saves the world. *Do I have all the answers?* No. *But will I always praise God?* Yes. Yes. Yes.

# ACKNOWLEDGMENTS

I am a believer in the power of the Holy Spirit to work with Holy Scripture when the holy people of God study and discuss Scripture together. To that end, I have been writing Bible study discussion questions for the local church for decades. I have added reflection questions to all the books I have written. For years I have written discussion questions for groups to wrestle with together alongside the content of the sermons at my local church. I've been humbled by the kind responses from individuals and groups of people who have found my questions thought-provoking and helpful. The God in the Neighborhood Bible Studies are my first attempt at a comprehensive, multivolume Bible study written for the local church for individual and group use. I'm grateful for the support and encouragement of so many who have made these Bible studies possible.

I'm grateful for the team at NavPress. As a high school student, I participated in The 2:7 Series discipleship course published by NavPress, and now, some thirty years later, I'm thrilled to be able to write a Bible study series to add to the NavPress catalog of discipleship resources. I appreciate the enthusiasm of David Zimmerman and Olivia Eldredge for this project. Since the first day I pitched the idea for a Bible study using the beauty and particularity of *The Message*, you have both given me unwavering support. Olivia, it has been a joy to work with you in the editorial process. You have a strong sense for how readers engage with the Scriptures and with my writing and reflection questions. Your keen insights and constant encouragement have made my writing better. Yay! Thanks to Elizabeth Schroll for your careful editorial work. It has been a true pleasure to work with you on this project.

Thank you also to the number of people who gave me feedback on titling and content for these studies. I'm grateful to Joe Beach, who shares a love for Eugene Peterson and *The Message*, for his suggestions and input. Thanks to fellow author and Bible study enthusiast Kat Armstrong for reading my first lesson and providing me with helpful feedback. Thanks also to the members of Word of Life Church in St. Joseph, Missouri, who attended many of the Bible studies I led during Advent 2023 and Eastertide 2024. Your discussions during those Bible studies gave shape to this series.

An unmistakable thank you is due to my wife, Jenni, who remains my faithful confidant and supporter. Thank you for giving up many Fridays when I was tucked away writing these Bible studies. Thanks to my sons, Wesley, Taylor, and Dylan. One book in this series is dedicated to each of you with a blessing. Each of you, in your own way, makes me so proud! Thank you to Maggie and my grandsons, Leo and Sam, for rounding out the Vreeland clan. I love you all so much. Thanks to my brother, Jeff, and my father, Ed, for all your support and for cheering me along as I write.

Finally, I'm deeply grateful for the impact Eugene Peterson has had on my life as a pastor, author, lover of Scripture, and follower of Jesus. My family gave me a copy of *The Message Devotional Bible* for Father's Day some time ago. While I had regularly referenced *The Message* over the years, I hadn't taken the time to read it daily until 2023 and 2024. I looked forward to my Bible reading during that season because *The Message Devotional Bible* not only provided me with Peterson's helpful contemporary translation but also offered notes from him along the way. I treasured spending those mornings with Eugene and his beautiful translation. These Bible studies, using *The Message*, are a way for me to extend my gratitude and to help, in a small way, to keep the life and legacy of Eugene Peterson alive. I love you, Eugene. Thanks for showing me the way.

# NOTES

## AS WE BEGIN | AN INTRODUCTION TO CRUCIFIXION

1. Eugene H. Peterson, "A Sort of Homecoming," *The Message Devotional Bible: Featuring Notes and Reflections from Eugene H. Peterson* (NavPress, 2018), 1069.
2. "Language and the way we use it in the Christian community are the focus of this conversation on the spirituality of language. Language, all of it—every vowel, every consonant—is a gift of God. . . . I want to tear down the fences that we have erected between language that deals with God and language that deals with the people around us. It is, after all, the same language." Eugene H. Peterson, *Tell It Slant: A Conversation on the Language of Jesus in His Stories and Prayers* (Eerdmans, 2008), 2, 4.

## LESSON 2 | LIKE A LAMB TAKEN TO BE SLAUGHTERED

1. Fleming Rutledge, *The Crucifixion: Understanding the Death of Jesus Christ* (Eerdmans, 2015), 197.
2. For examples of Job's friends accusing him of wrongdoing (and thus insinuating that he was to blame for the suffering he endured), see Job 11:13-20; 15:1-16; 22:1-11.
3. Robert Robinson, "Come, Thou Fount of Every Blessing," 1758. Public domain.

## LESSON 3 | THIS IS MY BLOOD

1. N. T. Wright, *The Day the Revolution Began: Reconsidering the Meaning of Jesus's Crucifixion* (HarperOne, 2018), 182.
2. Glenn Packiam, *Blessed Broken Given: How Your Story Becomes Sacred in the Hands of Jesus* (Multnomah, 2019).

## LESSON 4 | GOD'S LOVE ON THE LINE

1. Joseph M. Scriven, "What a Friend We Have in Jesus," 1855. Public domain.

## LESSON 7 | HIS WOUNDS, OUR HEALING

1. *The Book of Common Prayer* (Anglican Liturgy Press, 2019), 46.
2. *Book of Common Prayer*, 771.
3. Jesus said, "The Father and I are one" (John 10:30, NLT), and the church has historically defined that oneness as one "substance" or "being" (Greek word: *homoousios*) in the Nicene Creed. Per the words of

this creed, Eastern Orthodox and Protestant Christians all believe that Jesus is one being, essence, and substance with the Father. Augustine, in the fourth century, extrapolated from this doctrine that because of the unity between the Father and Son (and Spirit), the members of the Trinity work together without division. In *On the Trinity*, he writes, "As they are indivisible, so work indivisibly. This is also my faith, since it is the Catholic faith" (Augustine, *On the Trinity*, Book I, accessed August 26, 2025, https://www.newadvent.org/fathers/130101.htm). By "Catholic faith," he means "universal faith," as in the universal belief of all Christians. When the eternal Son of God joined us in death, descending to the abode of the dead to liberate the captives there, he did so with the Father and the Spirit, since the Trinity cannot be divided in any of their work.

## LESSON 8 | A DEATH THAT TRIGGERED LIFE

1. Thomas Aquinas, *Summa Theologiæ*, Prima Secundæ Partis 62.3, trans. Fathers of the English Dominican Province, accessed June 11, 2025, https://www.newadvent.org/summa/2062.htm#article3.